FORGIVE OR FORGET IT

Put the Stress on Success and Achieve Your Goals

Mark Peacock

Forgive or Forget It: Put the Stress on Success and Achieve Your Goals

Copyright © 2020 Mark Peacock

ISBN: 978-1-77277-351-4

All rights reserved. No portion of this book may be reproduced mechanically, electronically, or by any other means, including photocopying, without permission of the publisher or author except in the case of brief quotations embodied in critical articles and reviews. It is illegal to copy this book, post it to a website, or distribute it by any other means without permission from the publisher or author.

Limits of Liability and Disclaimer of Warranty
The author and publisher shall not be liable for your misuse of the enclosed material. This book is strictly for informational and educational purposes only.

Warning – Disclaimer
The purpose of this book is to educate and entertain. The author and/or publisher do not guarantee that anyone following these techniques, suggestions, tips, ideas, or strategies will become successful. The author and/or publisher shall have neither liability nor responsibility to anyone with respect to any loss or damage caused, or alleged to be caused, directly or indirectly by the information contained in this book.

Publisher
10-10-10 Publishing
Markham, ON   Canada

Printed in Canada and the United States of America

Table of Contents

Dedication	v
Foreword	vii
Acknowledgements	ix
Chapter One: Just Between You and Me	1
Chapter Two: Creating the Pathway to Success	5
Chapter Three: Focus	17
Chapter Four: Organization	25
Chapter Five: Relationships	45
Chapter Six: Generosity	57
Chapter Seven: Imagination	71
Chapter Eight: Visualization	79
Chapter Nine: Endurance	93
Chapter Ten: In the Meantime	105
About the Author	117

Dedication

To everyone who has fallen, got up again, and wants to fall less. You are not alone.

Foreword

Would you like an opportunity to shift how you view your current situation? Would you like to create success, and change your life forever?

If the answer to either, or both, of these questions is yes, then *Forgive or Forget It* is the book for you!

I first met author Mark Peacock at one of my 10-10-10 presentations, and I was pleasantly surprised and delighted to learn of his highly inventive "Forgive" method. Through this process I uncovered parts of myself that I would not have thought about from this perspective before. It has shifted how I view my own situation in life, and now you have the opportunity to change yours.

The "Forgive" method will challenge you to examine how you interact with your world, and how your perceptions can affect you in a profound way. Mark's creative approach to coaching you towards modifying your stress into success will help you to discover alternative ways of viewing age-old questions. Mark asks you to think about where you want to go, and what success looks like for you. And then he asks you to consider what stands in your way.

In addition, in a rare mix of vulnerability and practicality, Mark reveals some of the situations he has faced in the past, and continues to struggle with in his own journey towards personal achievement. In a straightforward, no-holds-barred fashion, Mark uses his signature "Forgive" method to guide you towards personal victory in whatever way you wish to achieve it. In a light comedic approach,

Mark offers a series of exercises to help you uncover what it is you want, as well as numerous practical suggestions to help you along the way.

I highly recommend *Forgive or Forget It*, and encourage you to dive in right away. You will not regret it.

Raymond Aaron
New York Times Bestselling Author

Acknowledgements

It is with the deepest gratitude that I wish to thank the many people who have been instrumental on my journey as both a coach and as the author of this book.

Thank you to my very first coach, Michelle Rothstein, who helped to light the pathway towards my success. I am very grateful for her sage guidance and innate ability to help me uncover my true desires. I really cannot believe how far I have come in five short years.

To the faculty at the Coach Training Program at Adler; in particular, Ann Reich, Bill Cyr, and Robin Altman, who mentored me along the way, I really cannot thank you enough. Thanks to Tony Gross, who accommodated all of my special requests and unique situations that allowed me to get here. Of course, a big thanks to all the wonderful colleagues and fellow students I met during my training, as well as a special thanks to Nancy Athey for her patience and willingness to partner with me, in order for us to both further our learning and solidify our skills.

In addition, I would like to express my gratitude to all of my coaching clients and the actors I worked with at the start of my career as a talent agent. It is through these early partnerships that I discovered my interest and desire to help others in this capacity.

A special thanks to the good folks at 10-10-10 Publishing, especially Liz Ventrella and Rosa Greco for their guidance with this project as well as Lisa Browning for her keen eye in correcting my grammatical shortcomings.

Forgive or Forget It

I would also like to thank my therapist, Robin Blake, for his undying patience as I continue on my journey towards self-awareness and peace within our chaotic world. As well, thank you to the many therapists who came before him; know that each one of you taught me something special, and helped me to become the man I am today. A special thank you to Jeffrey Smith, a terrific hypnotherapist who has really helped guide me towards a more serene existence, as well as deepen my awareness of visualization, and helped to incorporate it into my daily routine.

To Tracey Erin Smith, thank you for inspiring me to find alternate ways to tell my story; the catharsis and learning I gleaned from the Soulotheatre experience was incredible. Thank you to Robert Windisman and Michael Boyuk, for helping me to learn how to create in a collaborative fashion, and for never failing to make me laugh and sometimes cry. To Shawn Hitchins and Byron Fast, thank you for your inspiration and for showing me that it can be done.

To my present and former agents—Amy Stulberg at Vanguarde Artists; Sohrab Merchant at Characters Talent Agency; Sean Kaufmann, Sandra Gillis, and Rod Maxwell at Premier Artists—thank you for all the opportunities for growth you have offered, as well as an alternate point of view, and for teaching me how to overcome rejection.

To the folks I have encountered throughout my journey through the reality television world: Patricia Hollinger, who gave me my first opportunity, and went the extra mile to support me; Michael Terresigni, Kyle Martin, Charlotte Griffin, and Mark Lysakowski, on *The Amazing Race Canada,* who supported and believed in me, I owe you the deepest gratitude; Tanya and Mike at Architect Films, who have provided a warm supportive environment for me to grow; and to Jennifer Pratt, who has been exceptionally generous and kind to me.

Acknowledgements

Thank you to my immediate family members, especially Marika Gemma, who were my first teachers, as well as all of my chosen family and friends who have loyally supported me and listened to me try out my myriad of theories and practices throughout this process.

In particular, thank you to those that allowed me to experiment, including Helena Werren, Ken Kirkwood, Maggie Cassella, Linda Mitton, and Thomas Widstrand. And those who engaged in long discussions about coaching, meditation, and human interaction, including Laurie Arron, Steven Bates, Alan Moon, Fabio Fernandes, Madeleine Wong, Elida Schoght, Jennifer Town, Pascal Ethier, Daphne Fernandes, and the incredibly insightful Seth Poulin, who never failed to tell me the truth even when I didn't want to hear it. Thank you to Tove Rees, whose knowledge and willingness to engage in mutually therapeutic chats has been unbelievably helpful. I thank you all from the bottom of my heart.

To my champions and cheerleaders who believed in me even when I did not, and those who helped me along the way: J.C., John Garcia, Sue-Roz Baker, Amanda Johnston, Ernest Agbuya, Amanda Aman, Laura Brehaut, Danielle Waxer, Sam D'Alfonso, Stephen Belcourt, Derrick Burgess, Ken Aucoin, Ian Carpenter, Richard Chambers, Stuart Charlap, Peter Rusk, Melissa D'Agostino, Laura Exley, Susan Fisher, Alicia Flay, Ricky Hernden, Michele Hoffman, Ava Ellul, Florence James, Courtney Goldman, Shafik Kamani, Naqeeb Khan, Gordon Lamrock, JP Laroque, Mark Latter, Scott MacDonald, Leisa Peacock, Debbie Peacock, Barbara Scheffler, Jill Ross, Chrysoulla Srabian, Debra MacMillan, Caroline Papineau, Bill Sarman, Paulina Robak, Joe Jamieson, Paulette Sinclair, Nico Stagias, and George Kallika. Thank you for always being there for me, putting up with me, and making me feel special.

Finally, thank you to one of my oldest friends, Allen Braude, who on that day in May as we strolled across the Brooklyn Bridge, helped spark an idea in me that would change my life forever.

Thank you all.

Chapter One

Just Between You and Me

The very first thing I discovered on my initial day of coach training was that as a coach, you are never supposed to give advice or offer an opinion. Well, I was floored. After all, the whole reason I was looking into coaching in the first place was because years before, when I worked as a talent agent, my favorite part, beyond getting to show up to work whenever I felt like it, and organizing all the actors' head shots in alphabetical order on my wall, was offering up management advice to my roster. If that weren't enough to spurn me on, then the fact that all my friends kept saying, "You'd be so good at it!" made me believe that coaching was a natural fit for my already sharpened advice-spewing gifts.

My naivety led me to believe that this type of personal coaching was exactly the same as being an athletic coach, whereupon clients would present the areas of their life that they were struggling with, and then as the *coach*, I would offer solutions. I figured I had already had a ton of problems in my own life and, therefore, I was well equipped to offer my take on other people's difficulties. So the words, "a coach never gives advice or offers their opinion," were a rude awakening for me, and one that took some getting used to. What I learned is that the basic philosophy of coaching hinges on the premise that you as the client are always held creative, resourceful, and whole, which means that all the answers you seek already exist within you. My role is simply to coax, or *coach*, these answers out of you.

In my journey, I have also encountered a fair number of people that after I have explained what to do, immediately remark that this type of coaching relationship seems to be akin to that of a psychotherapist. Yes, there is a therapeutic element to the process, as coaching often poses difficult questions that can illicit emotional responses from you, but it is definitely not therapy. So in the interest of clarity around what coaching is and how it functions, I think it is important that I define how it compares to similar forms of interactions; that is, psychotherapy, mentoring, and consulting.

In general, the role of therapy is to uncover the motivations behind present behaviors that are impacting your life, and to try and heal these wounds. In effect, to look to the past for answers to present day problems, whereas in coaching, although it may refer to the past, the focus is to look forward to the future. However, if within the coaching process, your past wounds are discovered and need to be healed, then I as a coach might refer you to a therapist, as this is not my area of expertise, and I am simply not qualified to help you in this regard. Since there are many forms of psychotherapy available, I would work with you to help you determine the one that suits you best.

Now if you are looking for someone who is in a position that you would like to attain, and are seeking the answers in order for you to get there, then what you are looking for is a mentor and not a coach. My role is to help you define what it is you really want to achieve, and then help you design the route in order to get there—not answer your questions about how you can move into my position. In the coaching relationship, my career history is immaterial, as the basic principles of coaching apply no matter what your situation is. So whether you are a banker or a trapeze artist, your particular high wire act is just as easily coachable for me.

Along the same lines, I have found that often clients come to me looking for specific support and suggestions about their careers, business plans, and personal affairs. These clients will inevitably pose the question, "Well, you've been in the same boat—what would you do in my position?" If this is what you are looking for, then you are searching for a consultant, not a coach. Remember, when it comes to you and your life, within the coaching relationship, my opinion is not what is important; it is for you to create and for me to support.

However, this does not mean I do not have an opinion or have not learnt many things on my own tumultuous journey through this great adventure called life, and this is where this book comes in. Unlike a typical coaching session, here I share insight into what I have discovered along the way, and the various models that have helped me—that is, the practical example type, not the Tyra Banks kind, although I have been known to take advantage of Tyra's "smize" technique on occasion; it really does bring your face alive in photos. Ultimately, the purpose of *Forgive or Forget It* is to offer you suggestions and exercises on how you can explore your own personal aspirations and get the most from your efforts.

Once, on an online dating app, I was posed the question, "What is your net worth?" Although I knew exactly what this person was referring to, and once I got past being affronted, it led to a deeper question. After all, there are many ways you can choose to interpret this. Yes, there is the question of financial assets, but if you are the sum of your parts, then is not your self-worth constructed of what you have acquired but also of your potential? How do you choose to put value on your physical self, your talents, your abilities, and your dreams?

The truth is that many people never allow themselves the room to dream, but you have this ability, so why not explore it? What stands in your way to figure out what it is that you really want, and then go for it? What makes you hesitate? You can have so much if you just allow yourself to think it and then work towards it. My hope is that through this book, you will find some inspiration and practical suggestions in order for you to put your stress on success and work around the rest.

This is a workbook, a guide to help you achieve your goals and perhaps even your wildest imaginings. It is a compilation of the many things I have discovered along my journey towards greater self-awareness and increased productivity. Everything that I offer is something that I have tried or do on a regular basis. So, it is important to note that it is okay if some of the exercises do not resonate with you, if this is the case, then simply ignore them and move on. All of these suggestions are merely my opinion based on observation and experience, and are designed as a jumping off point to help you get started. So please take what works for you, and disregard what does not. As is anything in life, you will find that the amount that you gain is in direct proportion to what you give. It is your life, so the only person you are accountable to is you. This book can help you to shift your life but only if you decide to make it happen. Remember, positive change and growth is not a magic spell; it is just a lot of hard work and a witch's brew of imagination and practicality. So what do you really want out of your life? What are you willing to do in order to achieve it? More importantly, are you ready to have some fun?

Chapter Two

Creating the Pathway to Success

From Hoboken to Santa Fe

In order to achieve your goals, you first need to determine what it is you actually want to accomplish. This may sound obvious or even ridiculous, but many people maintain only a vague notion of what they really want and, as a result, never realize their true dreams. The more specific your goal, the more likely you will be able to attain it. This is simply because it is much easier to figure out the path when you know where you are going. If you were to go on a road trip from Hoboken, New Jersey to Santa Fe, New Mexico, would you just hop into your mini-van, point it east, and start driving? It's unlikely; you would either plot the route using a map (if you happen to be one of those people who still remembers how to use one), or punch your destination into your smart phone, and let the passive- aggressive dulcet tones of your GPS guide your way. The same principle applies on the journey towards personal and professional success.

Generally, one of the first exercises I do when I first meet with a new client is something called, "The Wheel of Life." This is a simple exercise that allows the client to start to figure out what areas of their life they want to focus on. First, you draw a circle and divide it into eight parts. Next, you label each piece of the pie with a category that you feel relates to your life. For example, I like to use the following categories:

- Home Environment
- Career
- Significant Other
- Friends & Family
- Health
- Fun and Recreation
- Money
- Personal Growth

Although it is important to note that you can use whatever categories or labels best suit your purpose or describe your life. For my clients, it looks like this:

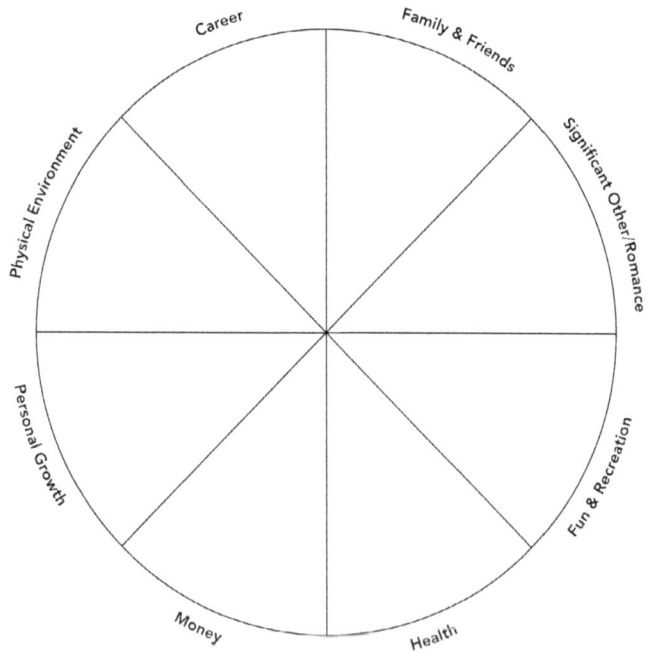

The next step is to use the centre as "0," and the outer edge as "10," and assign a number in between the two that you feel best represents how you would rate your level of satisfaction in this area of your life. Finally, place a dot on the number and then connect all the dots. So it looks something like this:

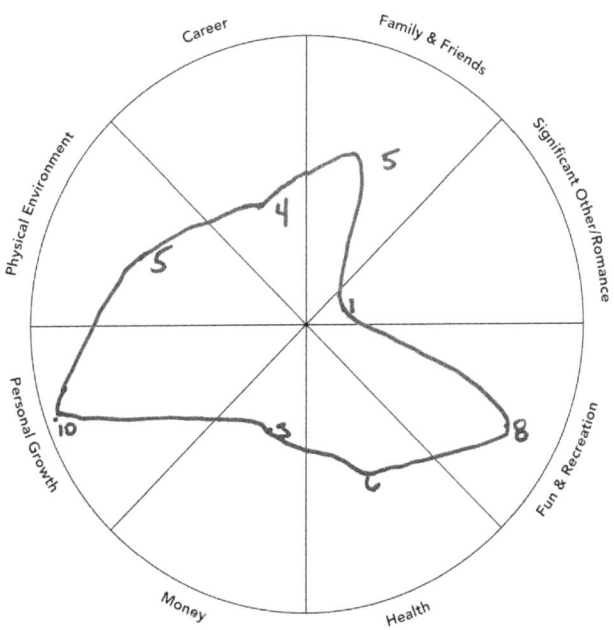

Notice that it is a rather irregular shaped wheel, and imagine how bumpy of a ride it would be if this were a wheel on your bike or car. Imagine the amount of tow trucks you would have to pay if you drove this wheel from Hoboken to Santa Fe. So obviously, this is not ideal, as the goal of your life is to not only maximize your enjoyment and live it to the fullest, but also to find an appropriate balance. So now try it yourself. What do you notice? How rough is your ride through life right now? What are the areas that you want to work on?

Now that you have a better sense of what it is you want to accomplish, the next question you need to ask yourself is, what does success look like for you? It's important to realize right from the get go that there are no right or wrong answers. There is no exam. There is no final grade. The only person you are accountable to is you. So what is it that you want to get out of your life? What do you want to achieve? What matters most to you? What excites you? What makes you want to jump out of bed in the morning, gulp down your coffee or kale smoothie (apparently some people like these sort of things), and start your day? I am fully aware that for some of you, this line of questioning may be akin to enquiring as to what it feels like to grow tomato plants in a Martian desert. So one method you can use to determine this is to think about a specific experience where you felt like you were at your best. What did it feel like? What about this experience appealed to you? How did it feel when you accomplished or finished the task?

A few years ago, I took a course in writing and performing a solo theatrical show. This is a type of theatre piece in which you explore a personal experience, construct a storytelling structure around it, and perform it. Some consider this to be an exhilarating notion, but for others, and definitely for me, the idea of getting up in front of an audience and sharing a personal story was absolutely terrifying—cue the onslaught of anxiety dreams where one is running naked through a shopping mall. However, I am also a bit of an emotional exhibitionist and not completely risk adverse, so I challenged myself to dive headfirst into this class, admittedly without checking the water very carefully. Mercifully, I had an instructor who was able to help keep me afloat throughout the process, and in the space of ten weeks, I wrote a twenty-minute piece about the recent death of my mother, with whom I had a somewhat contentious relationship. Although I felt reasonably secure in the text that I had written, as the performance date inched nearer, my anxiety grew exponentially. Night after night, I would wake at four am, plagued by an onslaught of self-generated doubts that rotated in my mind like a rickety Scrambler ride at one of those travelling carnivals. "What was I thinking?" "Why am I doing this?" "Who am I to share this story?" "What is that weird rolling sound coming from the neighbors above me? Do they sleep in a shopping cart?"

By the time the day of the show arrived, I was a certifiable mess. I stumbled through the dress rehearsal, I forgot large sections of dialogue, and I slipped back into my thirteen-year-old manner of suburban lipless mumbling that has taken me years of conscious speech work to overcome. It was horrifying, and one hour before the show, my instructor took me aside and told me it was okay if I just stood there, held the script in my hands, and read it aloud. I was crushed. Suddenly, I was jettisoned back to my university days as a clarinetist in the music program. Year after year, I auditioned to get into Master Class for performance; and each time, I was crippled by anxiety and consequently rejected, and as a result, mortified. However, in this situation, I had a choice: Do I succumb to my own feelings of inadequacy, and heed the advice of authority, or do I take a risk and go for it?

As the lights came up, I surveyed the crowd, their eyes alight with anticipation. I quickly clocked the nearest exits should I suddenly find it suddenly necessary to run out of the theatre screaming "fire" at the top of my lungs. Over the dull pounding of my heart, beating a hundred forty clicks per minute, I opened my mouth and began. Twenty-two and a half minutes later, it was over. I had shared my story, garnered a few laughs, and even a generous round of applause. I blushed, bowed, and left the stage. Only then did I finally allow myself the luxury of a full breath and a smile as I picked up my script that I had left in the wings. I had done it. I wasn't ready for an off-Broadway run, but I didn't feel I had to run out the back door either.

What I discovered from this experience was that I loved storytelling. Sure, I had always enjoyed good dinner party repartee where I could regale my friends with the oddball tales of my life. But this was different. It had a larger and deeper reach, and what was really exciting to me was that by sharing my story, both the good and the bad, I could help others who may have had a similar experience. Yes, it was a ton of hard work, but when I was in the thick of it, that barely crossed my mind. Also, the rush of pleasure I felt when I was done was also incredible. I became addicted. I wanted more, and I went on to expand the piece to a full seventy-five minute show that I have now performed a number of times.

When you examine a peak experience from your past, it helps to identify what is most important to you; that is, your core values. For me, I learned that authenticity, perseverance, organization, and giving back to others (generosity) are some of what I value the most. From here, I was able to dig into these values and look for more opportunities, and set appropriate goals where these could be explored. This has become my litmus for success; that is, to align my goals with my core values.

Exercise: Peak Experience

Okay, now it's your turn. Think of a peak experience in your life where you feel you were operating at your best. It could be a sports, arts, family, job, or education related situation, as long as at the end you felt like you accomplished what you set out to do, and felt fantastic while you did it. Now, either write it down or share it with a friend or family member. From here, determine what core values you accessed in order to achieve success. Now think of what activities align with these values. Ask yourself: What do you want more of in your life? Who do you want to be? How do you want to be remembered?

This simple exercise is great for helping to sketch a path towards success. It can also be used as a reference if at times you begin to lose sight of where it is you want to head, as the road to success is of course never smooth. When you embark on your journey, you will most likely encounter detours, rocky roads, twists and turns, so it is important to keep yourself as open and flexible as possible. However, what you will discover is that if you remain in touch with your values as you work towards your goals, you are guaranteed to experience the feeling of success, regardless of the outcome. The key is how you choose to handle the roadblocks that you will inevitably hit along the way.

Wake Up and Sell the Coffee

Ever have one of those days where no matter what you do, you are stymied at every turn? You know, the type of day where you have a job interview at nine AM and wake up thirty minutes before it because you set your alarm for seven PM instead of seven AM?

Almost all of us have had some form of that kind of day at some point in our lives. This is why the clichés, *"Mama said there would be days like this,"* and some form of *"Keep calm, carry on,"* grace millions of t-shirts and mugs around the world. These kinds of minor incidents are troublesome and can definitely stand in the way of achieving your goals. However, these types of incidents are generally the exception, not the rule; unless of course you are the hapless hero of an early 90's sitcom with a neighbor named *"Kramer."* What is more important is to look below the surface of these unfortunate coincidences and examine the thoughts that accompany them. A close examination of your thought process during stressful situations will give you insight into the real obstacles that stand in the way of your success.

For instance, I have many of these types of days— generally one or two a month if I'm being completely honest—and what I have discovered is that my attitude is what colors my perception of them. Our lives can be boiled down to a series of experiences that we perceive through our own lens. We filter our perceptions through past experiences, which then inform our point of view. In my case, I have a long history of beating myself up. So when faced with a stressful situation or when something does not go the way I want it to, my first thought is, "It's my fault; I deserve this bad thing." I have a habit of blaming myself, and I love to indulge in self-pity—it's like chocolate for the dark part of my soul.

In addition, since I have always struggled with self-esteem, I am often plagued by self-doubt. My brain can often get caught in a continuous loop of tunes with titles like: *"You Can't Do It"*; *"They're All Gonna Laugh at You"*; *"Who Do You Think You're Kidding?"* and my personal favorite, *"You Suck at Everything and You Ain't Never Gonna Succeed."* It's like the set list for a B-grade country singer. The unfortunate thing for me is that quite often, the closer I am to success, the louder these familiar refrains play.

Years ago, when I graduated from the Canadian Film Centre, I was the only person in my class to garner interest from a production company for my original TV sitcom concept. It was a huge honor, and although I was thrilled when the head of development from the production company contacted me, I was also absolutely petrified. When the morning of the meeting arrived, I put on my best, *"I'm creative but not completely bonkers"* outfit, hopped in my car, and headed to the trendy coffee shop where we were to meet, with a name something along the lines of "Wake Up and Sell the Coffee."

I took a seat and proceeded to check my watch obsessively as my heart rate ever so slowly increased to near cardiac arrest levels. By the time the executive arrived (twenty minutes late), I was nearly unconscious from terror and could barely croak out a timid, "Hello, nice to meet you." Although the executive was pleasant enough, I could not soothe the internal savage fear beast that shook me to the core. So after pleasantries, a brief diatribe about the state of Canadian television, and their enthusiastic response to my script, the executive asked me point blank, "So, can you see your idea on television?" To which I immediately hung my head and meekly replied, "Oh, gosh no, it's not very good."

Needless to say, I never heard from this production company ever again, and why would I? After all, if I didn't believe in myself, why would I expect anyone else to? I really was asking too much, I wanted this executive to refute me, and boost my self-esteem for me—in short, do the work for me. This was not only unrealistic but also a tall order for a stranger to fulfill. Although very painful, this was also very educational. Clearly, I had a lot of work to do on my inner critic if I was ever going to succeed.

When you take a heartfelt look at what stands in your way on the journey towards creative success, and look deeper, you may discover that you have mechanisms that can sabotage your progress. How do you react when you are under stress? What gets in your way? What obstacles do you put in place for yourself, either consciously or unconsciously?

Exercise: What Stands in Your Way?

Think of an experience in your life where you feel you were not operating at your best. Now, either write it down or share it with a friend or family member. What happened? What stood in your way? How did you feel at the moment? What were the main thoughts that informed your reactions or behaviors? What did you choose to do at the time? What were your actions or non-actions? What were you afraid of?

As you work towards success it is normal to experience complications and this exercise helps to identify some of the obstacles that are specific to your situation. One of the more common emotions that create considerable grief for many people is fear. It is an innate part of our genetic make-up, buried deep in our primal brain. Although originally designed to protect us from potential death on the Savannah or in the rainforest, in modern times these flight or fight responses can often get in our way. So it is necessary to figure out what you are frightened of so that you can forgive yourself for it and move past it.

Forgive or Forgo

Now that you have a clearer sense of your core values and what success means to you, how do you want to focus your energy? In order to achieve the life you truly desire, you need to start to take steps in that direction. What do you want your life to look like? What are the specific goals you want to accomplish?

Forgiveness is an immensely important part of any type of success. It is only through forgiveness and understanding of our own shortcomings or mistakes that we can move past them. In addition, by forgiving ourselves we can truly find joy in what we do, and in turn experience the feeling of true success. Furthermore, if we break down the word *forgive* in two parts—*for* and *give*—it is then easy to see how pardoning ourselves in order to achieve our goals is simultaneously for *giving* to others and ourselves. It also provides the basis of a mnemonic for a technique that has helped me to achieve my goals.

The "For Give" Technique:

- Focus
- Organization
- Relationships
- Generosity
- Imagination
- Visualization
- Endurance

So let's take a look at each one of these so that you can start to change your outlook and move one step closer to achieving your goals.

Chapter Three

Focus

The Big Leagues

A few years ago, I was working on a high profile competitive cooking show in an on-set position that many aspiring writers in the television industry would covet. Essentially, I was responsible for everything that the host said, which meant I often had to write lines "on the fly" and feed them to him over a microphone into his ear piece, while simultaneously the executive producer shouted instructions into my ear to give to him. This was an incredible challenge because having someone yell at you while at the same time you are trying to talk, is a little bit like trying to pat your head and rub your belly at the same time. Imagine trying to give coherent directions to a cab driver while your child shrieks about how Johnny stole their peanut butter and jelly sandwich at lunch, at the top of their lungs, into your right ear.

Obviously, it was the type of job that required me to be on my toes constantly, but even worse (especially for my personality type), it was the kind of situation where the entire cast and crew could witness every mistake I made. This made me feel incredibly vulnerable and, as a result, I spent each day with my stomach tied up in knots of anxiety, which only served to decrease my effectiveness and increase the amount and frequency of errors. For instance, the time I asked the host to say, "Chefs, now that you've knocked it out of the culinary park, it's time to pitch your dishes to the judges," and one of the celebrity chefs turned to him and said in a loud voice, on the completely silent set, "Wow, who wrote that? Clearly, they're not fit for the big leagues." And cut. Cue the uncomfortable coughs as my cheeks flushed a brilliant scarlet.

You see, ever since I was a child, I have always suffered from what I term the, "I could do it when no one was watching, I swear!" syndrome. My earliest memory of this was when I was about seven years old and I was learning to ride a bike. I remember that I would manage to find my balance, and begin to sail down the street, but as soon as I said, "Hey! Look at me!" I would immediately fall off the bike or slam into a tree trunk. Eight pairs of skinned knees and elbows over two weeks later, and you quickly learn that it is a bad idea for anyone to watch you do anything challenging...ever.

Now, almost forty years later, I found myself in basically a similar situation. Sure, the details were different, but the core experience was exactly the same. Luckily, over the length of my contract, my confidence slowly grew, and in conjunction, so did my ability. However, one thing that did not evolve was my job satisfaction, as my anxiety remained an uncomfortable constant. I now had a choice: Do I continue down the same career path, or do I actively seek other opportunities?

Mercifully, at the time, a friend of mine was in close contact with a personal and professional coach. So with a little bit of skepticism and a whole lot of low expectations, I set up a meeting with her. After she dutifully listened to me outline a long list of gripes and complaints about my present situation, she very simply asked, "Well, you clearly have a good sense of what you don't want... so what is it you do want?"

Too often, you get mired in your disappointments and regrets, and you lose sight of the fact that in this society, you are likely to have the privilege of choice. Unfortunately, you also generally have a myriad of self-imposed expectations and restrictions set in place that you may or may not be aware of. So where do you begin to choose a focus in order to facilitate desired change? One of the first exercises my coach encouraged me to experiment with was to create my own, personal Ultimate Wish List—a record of everything I wanted from my life if I could do anything I wanted, and if there were absolutely no restrictions; that is, financial, familial responsibilities, environmental restrictions, etc. The point was to allow my imagination the freedom to explore and envision what a life of possibilities might look like for me.

Exercise: The Ultimate Wish List

Grab a piece of paper and a pen, and give yourself permission to fantasize about every possible thing you want out of life. In this arena, there are no restrictions, as time, money, age, and resources are not an issue. This is your chance to write down everything you have ever wanted to have or achieve. Go for it, and really allow yourself to daydream about what your life can offer and what you think will really bring you joy.

Suggestion: Find a comfortable space and give yourself enough time to do this exercise, and truly allow your imagination to run wild. This is not the type of exercise you should try while rushing to work or standing in the supermarket line-up.

What I discovered when I completed my list was that although there were several items that were never going to come true (i.e. at age forty-seven, it was a little late for me to star in the title role of Mozart's opera, *Don Giovanni*, at Carnegie Hall), it did help me identify areas I could explore that might give me a similar type of satisfaction. Yes, perhaps it was too late for me to become a professional opera singer, but that didn't mean I couldn't take singing lessons or perhaps perform with a local choir or in a community musical production. Essentially, the list helped me to narrow down what excited me most in life, where my true passions lay, and what I believed would make me the most happy, which in turn aided me in identifying what direction I wanted to head in and what goals I wanted to achieve.

Another exercise that can help you to figure out what it is you want to accomplish, or how you want your life to look, is the Dream Day tool. This is a very simple task where you imagine your ideal day in the not too distant future, and how you are spending your time.

Exercise: Dream Day

Again, take a piece of paper and a pen, or your lap top, find a comfortable space, and give yourself plenty of time to relax and daydream. Close your eyes and imagine yourself five years from now and it is the perfect day. What are you doing? What does the environment around you look like? How do you feel? Who are you with? What kind of conversations are you having? What is on your mind? What are you excited about? What have you accomplished? Remember that there are no right or wrong ways to execute this exercise. I had a client who chose to write theirs as a narrative, but you can also do it in point form, or as your imaginary schedule/time table for the day. Be creative and have fun with it. It is very important that you register that this is a great day, one where you feel deeply satisfied and contented.

One final exercise, that some of my clients have found incredibly useful to figure out how to focus their energy, is the Lifetime Achievement Award Speech. This is where you imagine that you are about to receive an award, and someone you admire greatly explains to the audience everything you have contributed to your industry and the people in your life. Personally, I imagined a dewy-eyed Sally Field standing in front an entire audience filled with television professionals. When I hit the stage, and as I lean in to accept my honorary Emmy and give her the obligatory kiss on the cheek, she whispers in my ear, "That's right, they like you; they really, really like you." Sally then, turns to the audience and steals my thunder by bursting into her signature "tears at the drop of a dime" act.

Exercise: The Lifetime Achievement Award

Think of someone you admire greatly. It can be a colleague, a family member, a celebrity, or anyone who deeply inspires you. Now imagine that they are about to give a speech to an audience full of people you admire and wish to impress, or care about. What do you want this person to say about you? What have you accomplished? What are the values you have brought? How have you had an effect on your immediate environment? Who are you in the world? Write all of these thoughts down and then read it aloud while you look into a mirror, or have someone read to you. How does it feel to hear these words spoken about you? What does it say about who you are and what you want to accomplish in your lifetime?

If you commit to one or (ideally) all three of these exercises, it can help you to identify what it is that actually makes you happy. Examine them closely; what stands out for you? What themes do you notice? What are the important elements that you want to have more of in your life? What pieces are missing from your present life? How would it feel if you started to incorporate more of these items into your life?

What I discovered from these three exercises was that certain themes made themselves very apparent. For example, I learned that I craved variety in my day-to-day life, and that I desired an equal balance of alone time and social time. Furthermore, I determined that what was missing from my life was being of assistance to others. I realized that as well as creating a legacy for myself, it was also important to me to help others to achieve their goals. From here, in conjunction with my coach, I was able to outline a four-pronged approach to my career. In addition to continuing to build my business as a writer, producer, and performer, I decided to also incorporate personal and professional coaching into my life. This was an element that I did not even realize I wanted until I went through this process. Now I had a direction I wanted to go and all I had to do was make it happen.

There by the Grace of a Higher Power Go I

When I was training to become a coach, during one of my in- class sessions, the facilitator asked us what kind of approach or strategy we employed when we set out to achieve a goal. We were presented with three options:

- Set the goal, break down step by step what you need to do in order to achieve this goal, and then take the first step. Adjust the plan if necessary.

- Set the goal, and just get started in the right direction. Take the first step and continually assess and adjust as you move forward.

- Set the goal, and then catch the opportunities as they present themselves, without a linear plan.

We were then asked for a show of hands of which we thought was the best strategy and the one we were mostly likely to use. Personally, I thought this was a no-brainer as it seemed quite obvious to me that clearly the first choice was the logical option. After all, how could you achieve a goal if you did not first plan out the necessary steps to take? So at the sound of "number one?" my hand proudly shot up as a huge superior grin spread across my face. However, when I looked around the room, only one other person also had their hand in the air, waving madly like a sweat hog on *"Welcome Back Kotter."* I was flabbergasted, as I thought everyone would obviously operate this way, but apparently not, as the majority chose options two or three.

This was a complete eye opener for me since I am the type of guy who is a linear thinker almost to the point of obsessive-compulsive disorder. I am so enamored with organizing stuff that I color code my closet, and my bookshelves are first divided into genre and then organized alphabetically by author. I basically have to resist the temptation to alphabetize my pantry—as it is, I like to "face" all the food items so the interior of my kitchen cupboards look like the shelves at the grocery store.

So you can imagine the look on my face when I discovered that one of my colleagues actually purchased an automobile before she even had a license. I was also completely shocked when another person, who identified most strongly with the third strategy, explained that they had no idea how they had morphed from an education in recreational development into becoming a marketing executive for one of the largest entertainment corporations in the world. Their self-pronounced approach to their own career planning was, "There by the grace of God go I."

The point is that there are no right or wrong ways of the approach you take in order to achieve your goals. In fact, most of my colleagues felt that they employed a bit of each technique, and it fluctuated depending on the situation. The important thing is for you to be aware of how you operate when you want to move forward. Of the three strategies, which one do you best identify with? How does this help you achieve your goals? How can you use it to serve you best? What needs to fall into place?

Forgive or Forget It

Now that you hold a stronger sense of what is important to you and what it is you want to achieve, how do you want to direct your energy? What kind of life do you want to live? What are the goals you want to achieve? It is important to determine this so you can move forward and figure out a way to turn your dreams into a reality. If you are ready and know where it is you want to go, then let's move on and start to design an action plan in order to get you there.

Chapter Four

Organization

Marie Kondo, You Ain't Got S**t on Me

When it comes to organization, I'm lucky, as it is something that I actually get a kick out of. Some people like to knit, others like to cook, and some like to play volleyball—admittedly, that one I do not understand, because it really just makes my hands sting like I've just shoved them in a toaster on Bagel setting. Me? I like to make lists—lots of lists. I have lists of all the movies I've seen. I have a list of all the books, movies, and television I want to consume. There are lists of the restaurants I want to try, places I've been, places I want to go, people I've met, people I want to meet, and of course, a comprehensive list of my lists.

Personally, since I think it is fun to organize, if a guest ever opens up my medicine cabinet they will immediately notice that not only have I color coded my sundries, but they are also in alphabetical order. I used to wonder if this propensity for order is genetic, as I grew up in a home where my dad vacuumed daily, and my mother lined her bookshelves with Reader's Digest Condensed Books that were organized by date of release. However, my older sister did not share this same sensibility. Whereas my room looked like the display showcase in the children's section of IKEA, my sister's bedroom closely resembled a crime scene out of an episode of Law & Order SHU (Special Hoarders Unit). In fact, when she finally moved out, my dad uncovered five teacups that had long been on the missing pottery list, along with a snow shovel and an unopened can of Campbell's tomato soup that had expired three years prior. Who knew soup expired?

I think that as a child, I unconsciously figured out that for me, organization meant control, and since I found the external world extremely chaotic, the one place that I could exert influence was my bedroom. This is a pattern that I have continued to develop and maintain over the years. In fact, if I'm truly being honest, I only feel comfortable in my home when everything is in its exact proper place; that is, if the cutlery all faces the same direction in the drawer, and tea towels sit at exact lengths as they hang off the stove handle.

I have come to accept and appreciate this quality about myself, even if it means I have to weather the occasional comment about me living in a model/staged home, or at worst, a query about what kind of medication I take for my obsessive compulsive disorder (the latter of which comes from my sister). However, for me, I have discovered that a balanced approach to organization can decrease stress and allow you to refocus your energy so you can put the emphasis on success. Let's look at this a little more closely.

Time (Clock of My Heart)

> *"In time, it could have been so much more...*
> *the time is precious I know..."*
> Culture Club (1982)

Time is an incredibly valuable resource, and generally one that most people feel they can never get enough of. How many times have you said or heard someone else say, "There are just not enough hours in the day," or "I would love to, but I just don't have the time." Clearly, one of the most difficult things most of us in our present society have to learn is how to properly manage our time in a way that best serves our needs. Since there are countless books written on this particular subject, I will not delve too deeply into the nitty gritty of time management, other than offer my own unique perspective on how I have learned to tackle this timeless and time consuming issue.

One of the things I have found most effective in my efforts to best manage my own time was to answer that age-old question of "Where does it go?" In order to achieve this, first I had to determine how I was actually spending my time (pretty basic stuff, eh? #obvious). The way I accomplished this was to simply write out what activities I engaged in, Monday through Sunday, and for how long, in a timetable not unlike the ones I used in high school. However, I do admit that I had to fight through my own resistance, as the mere mention of anything high school related often triggers anxiety-ridden memories of parachute pants, Rubik's Cubes, and moody Tears for Fears lyrics about everyone wanting to rule the world. At one point during the process, I swear I caught a whiff of the Drakkar Noir that used to saturate my Polo shirts from that period—collar up, of course.

Since at the time I was working from home and therefore responsible for my own schedule, the timetable looked like what is displayed on page 28:

As I examined my schedule, this is what struck me:

- I generally had a late start to most of my days.
- I was spending an inordinate amount of time constantly checking, rechecking, and dealing with email and social media. (I mean, do I really need to know that my friend, Karen, fed her cat organic food, in the middle of my supposed workday?)
- The schedule was erratic and unfocused.

	MONDAY	TUESDAY	WEDNESDAY	THURSDAY	FRIDAY	SAT/SUN
9:00-10:00	Morning Routine	N/A	N/A	Morning Routine	Morning Routine	FREE DAY
10:00-11:00	Email/Admin	Morning Routine	Morning Routine	Email/Admin	Email/Admin	
11:00-12:00	Write: Spec	Edit: Web Series	Email/Admin	Write: Spec	Coaching Client	
12:00-1:00	Write: Spec	Email/Admin	Write: Spec	Email/Admin	Write: Spec	
1:00-2:00	Email/Admin Lunch	Lunch	Coaching Client	Gym	Email/Admin Lunch	
2:00-3:00	Gym	Write: Spec	Email/Admin Lunch	Rehearsal	Lunch	
3:00-4:00	Coaching Client	Email/Admin	Gym	Email/Admin	Gym	
4:00-5:00	Email/Admin	Gym	Rehearsal	Edit: Web Series	Coaching Client	
5:00-6:00	Rehearsal	Email/Admin	Edit: Web Series	Email/Admin	Email/Admin	
6:00-7:00	Email/Admin		Email/Admin			

Since at the time I had four separate projects on the go, I needed to figure out a way to improve my efficiency, or else I would never get anything finished. My first step was to extend my working day by an additional hour. Step two was to configure my activities so that I reduced the amount of time I wasted in between them. I also reduced the amount of times I allowed myself to check my email and correspondence, restricting it to only the beginning, middle, and end of my day. Finally, I moved two of my coaching clients to the end of the day, and configured the other two so that I reduced the amount of time I lost due to travel. My new schedule looked like this:

Organization

	MONDAY	TUESDAY	WEDNESDAY	THURSDAY	FRIDAY	SAT/SUN
8:00-9:00	Morning Routine	Morning Routine	Morning Routine	Morning Routine	Morning Routine	FREE DAY(s) Errands/Admin
9:00-10:00	Admin/Email	Admin/Email	Admin/Email	Admin/Email	Admin/Email	
10:00-11:00	Write: Spec	Write: Spec	Write: Spec	Write: Spec	Write: Spec	
11:00-12:00	Write: Spec	Write: Spec	Write: Spec	Write: Spec	Write: Spec	
12:00-1:00	Gym	Gym	Gym	Gym	Gym	
1:00-2:00	Lunch/Email	Lunch/Email	Lunch/Email	Lunch/Email	Lunch/Email	
2:00-3:00	Edit: Web Series	Edit: Web Series	Edit: Web Series	Edit: Web Series	Edit: Web Series	
3:00-4:00	Write: Stage	Write: Stage	Write: Stage	Write: Stage	Coaching Client	
4:00-5:00	Rehearsal	Rehearsal	Rehearsal	Rehearsal	Coaching Client	
5:00-6:00	Email/Reading	Email/Reading	Email/Reading	Email/Reading	Email/Reading	
6:00-7:00	Coaching Client		Coaching Client			

I also chose to maintain my rule that Saturday and Sunday were free days, and the days when I would deal with household chores and administration. I am a strong believer that even if you work for yourself, and make your own schedule, you are still entitled to a weekend. Not only does this give you a much needed break but also lessens the amount of resentment you feel for the rest of the world.

Obviously, the way you design your schedule is a very personal thing, and this was one that worked for me. However, I know colleagues who schedule all their meetings on the same day, and others who do all their administrative work, invoicing, etc. on Mondays, and others who are really pressed for time, who go so far as to prepare all their lunch meals or orders in advance so that it's one less thing they have to think about. There are also the extreme cases that wear the same style outfit all the time like a McDonald's uniform or Jeff Goldblum in *The Fly*, because it is one less thing they have to make a decision about. So the question becomes, what works best for you? How do you want your daily and weekly routines to look?

It's also very important to recognize that I use this type of schedule as a primary guide, as situations always arise that conflict. So you need to maintain a certain amount of flexibility, and to remember that your own personal schedule is a base upon which you can build how you want to spend your time. In addition, this type of schedule can be used even if you have a full time job that is externally scheduled, as it can help you focus your pre and post working hours, especially if you are contemplating shifting your career.

Exercise: Design Your Own Schedule

This is a three-step process and ironically a bit time consuming but ultimately quite useful.

Step One:
Map out how you spend your time from Monday to Sunday. You can design it any way that works best for you. I find the chart or timetable format is easiest for me to visualize, but do it in a manner that you are most comfortable with.

Step Two:
Examine your timetable, and ask yourself the following questions:

- Where am I losing time?
- How much time do I lose travelling from activity to activity?
- How I can reconfigure the activities so I am not wasting time?
- What activities can I configure (i.e. the two birds/one stone rule)?
- What activities can I eliminate completely?
- What activities do I really want to add?
- What changes or steps can you take so your schedule is more in line with what you want out of life?
- Overall, what have you discovered about how you use your time?

Step Three:
Redesign your schedule in response to your answers to the above questions. How do you feel about your new schedule?

Stop and Go Traffic on the Information Highway

I remember the first time I heard the phrase, "the information highway." It was 1994, and I was working at the Academy of Canadian Film and Television as the box office manager for the Gemini Awards (the Canadian Emmys), and they were having a conference to introduce this brand new technology. I, of course, paid absolutely no attention, as I was busy trying to accommodate Ernie Coombs' (aka Mr. Dress-Up) ticket requests. I do remember, however, glibly stating, "Information highway? The inter what? Oh, please, it'll never stick." It's a good thing I don't moonlight as a psychic, because my gifts are clearly lacking in this area.

It didn't even cross my mind again until about 1997, when one of the talent agents at the agency I worked with, whose tendencies towards the overdramatic would be an understatement, told me wide-eyed that we were about to install this new computer thing in which you could look up information and communicate using the "World Wide Web." Man, was she excited. I was not; and I was even less so when I discovered it was going to utilize one of our five phone lines, take seven minutes to connect, and even longer to open a word document, let alone a jpeg of someone's head shot.

This was also when I got my first email address, which admittedly I still use to this very day, although I really should update it, as monkeyraverboy@aol.com is not exactly the most professional address or age appropriate moniker for a man my age. I was also very resistant to the idea of email, as I thought it was way easier to pick up my purple cell phone (about the size of a size-9 converse hi-top) and call someone than it was to type out a message. And if I needed to send a document, we had a fax machine. What more could you ask for?

However, these days, communication has progressed to such a level that talking on the phone seems like something a 1950's housewife did. Ask a millennial what an answering machine is, and you'll be greeted by a blank stare—and email is now for the elderly. Social media and apps like Snap Chat and Instagram have even eclipsed such old technology as Facebook, Messenger, and even in some cases, texting. We now have more ways than ever to communicate information with each other. This also means we have even more ways to confuse, misinterpret, lose, and forget messages. Therefore, we have to be even more diligent and organized in our efforts to maintain our correspondence and contact with other.

This is especially important when it comes to your business and business contacts. For example, because clearly my original email is not the one I want to employ for my business, I now have two email accounts—one for business and one for personal correspondence. However, I am still guilty of occasionally forgetting and using

Organization

my personal account for business, and depending on what project is consuming my time, I can forget to check the business one. In fact, I once went six weeks without checking it over the winter, only to discover that I missed an opportunity to work on a project that was of greater interest than the contract that was now consuming my time. Lesson learned. I now make a list of all the venues I need to check for messages daily, which includes personal email, business email, texts, Facebook, and Instagram; and every morning, I make sure I go through all of them, and enjoy the feeling as I tick them off my to-do list.

Here are some other suggested techniques I employ in order to ensure I don't miss anything:

- Keep all of your email inboxes empty – I know, crazy, right? Your goal at the end of every day is to make sure that you have read, and answered, deleted, or most importantly, filed, every email you've received that day. This way, you can ensure that you haven't missed anything and/or have dealt with each one in a timely and appropriate fashion.

- Create email folders – In order to make sure you keep your email inbox empty, file the ones you need to save, into the appropriate folders, and delete the rest. You might have folders for taxes, invitations, work related topics, etc. This way, you can track everything and never lose any important information in a continual daily whirlwind of correspondence.

- Make a daily "to contact" list – To ensure that you do not forget anyone, and to maintain all your work and social contacts, make daily "contact" lists and weekly contact lists that you can then track in your calendar.

- Eliminate spam – Now that the law has changed and you can easily remove yourself from spam mail-outs, Do It! After all, do you really need all those alerts from such and such because you once bought a grilled cheese maker online? Clear out the electronic clutter, and simplify your life.

- Use several email addresses – Personally, I don't use more than two, as my memory is fading, so if I had more than that, I would forget to check it. However, I know of people who have a designated email solely for their friends, their work, their online shopping, etc.

- Keep your text list as empty as possible – Do you really need to keep all your text conversations about how your boss, Marnie, has a really bad habit of saying "um" before every thought? "Um" …no, you don't.

Spatial Awareness

Recently, I visited a friend ostensibly to help her hang art in her new apartment. Once she decided where she wanted to hang each piece, I told her to grab some nails and her tool kit and we could start. Proudly, she pulled out a small brown paper bag with exactly eleven nails in it. I quickly surmised that she had ten pieces of art, so ten nails and one for safety. Naturally, I congratulated her on her preciseness, and then asked for her hammer, at which point she whipped off one of her shoes and handed it to me. When I looked at her confused, she blushed deeply and admitted that she had followed the instructions given by Marie Kondo in her organizational book, *The Life-Changing Magic of Tidying Up*, and after holding her hammer to her heart, had decided that she felt no love for her tool kit, and had therefore sold it for five dollars at a yard sale prior to her move.

There is definitely something to be said for the recent cultural zeitgeist of "decluttering." After all, thanks to the success of television

Organization

shows like *Hoarders,* no one wants to be the person who has to be airlifted out of their home after being buried under an avalanche of old Best Buy flyers and Mennonite quilts. However, moderation is also necessary, as even though I don't have any particular strong heartfelt feelings for my dinner plates, boy oh boy, do they come in handy when I have a dinner party or when I decide I don't want to eat pizza straight out of the box. In my opinion, the most important question to ask yourself is, does your environment create or alleviate stress?

In my late thirties, after my significant relationship ended and I moved into an apartment on my own, I was for the first time in a position without roommates or a partner, where I could set up my home anyway I liked. I was extremely excited as I no longer had to compromise; and moreover, I could control every aspect of my environment. So I quickly busied myself with stacking my Tupperware from largest to smallest, alphabetizing my CD collection (remember those?), and color coding my closet. When I was done, I looked around and I was so proud—everything was exactly the way I wanted it.

However, I recognize that not everyone has this luxury, and that most of us have to learn to compromise within their homes, and even more so at their work place. So if you cannot control your entire home or office, what is the one space within it that you can? Is it your own personal office? Your bedroom? Your desk? What area of your environment is exclusive to you, and how can you design it so that you feel comfortable in it? And if you do not have a space, is there a way that you can create one?

Exercise: Design Your Own Creative Space

In order to achieve your goals, you need to have a space that is a hundred percent yours and that you feel good about. It does not have to be a huge space like a studio or an office; it could simply be a corner of a room, or your desk. What space you choose is of course completely up to you.

Step One:
Stake your claim. Find the space that you want to make your own.

Step Two:
Organize the space the way you like it. After all, if you live in a shared home or work situation, this is one space that you are allowed to exert complete control over. Now, if neat is your thing, then by all means de-clutter; organize your papers, go to a store like IKEA, Staples, or Binz, and go wild. They have tons of devices and boxes to help put all the odds and ends together.

Step Three:
Personalize it. For some of you, that may mean hanging a piece of art that inspires you, or placing a few items around within arm's reach that make you smile or give you comfort. You can also hang your credentials on the wall, or write inspirational sayings on stickies. What you choose does not matter, and should not matter to anyone else but you, as long as it creates an environment that you want to be in—a place where you feel you can focus and be creative.

Finally, remember that the most important element of this exercise is that you make the space your own, as it should serve as a retreat that inspires your deepest creativity, and as a result, your highest productivity.

Money, Money, Money, Must Be Funny... In a Rich Man's World

For the first ten years of my working life, I struggled to pay my rent each month, and subsisted on discount pasta with canned sauce. I would like to say that I was a struggling artist, but really, that would be overestimating my artistic abilities. The truth is that from nineteen to thirty-five, I racked up nine years of post-secondary education, two degrees, one professional certificate, along with an aborted attempt at theatre school, and all the debt that goes with it. So in my late thirties, when I finally got my first good paying job, I went a little crazy. In fact, I thought I was rich. I wasn't; it was just that I had been poor for so long that my perception was skewed. So I bought expensive dinners for my friends, and I purchased designer clothing. I even went as far as hiring a personal assistant to procure my internet/cable services, as well as help me assemble my new IKEA furniture (in my defense, I am pretty hopeless at that sort of thing, so I still consider that bit money well spent).

This casualness with money carried on for about a year, until the following April when my accountant did my taxes and informed me that I owed a huge amount to the government. I was flabbergasted. After all, I was self-employed. Was I not entitled to massive write-offs? Apparently not, and moreover, since I was so swept up in the thrill of a significant and regular pay check, I had forgotten to take into account that as an independent contractor, they were not deducting any income tax. So now I was slapped with a tax bill that was approximately thirty percent of what I had earned that year, with absolutely nothing put aside to cover it. This was a painful lesson to learn, and changed my approach to money forever.

As penance, from that moment on, I began to track every cent that I spent (see above re: lists) so that I could see where my money was going, and make the necessary adjustments to ensure that I would remain financially soluble. In addition, I also began to put aside at least thirty percent of each pay period in order to cover my taxes for the next year, as well as pay off my credit card and make regular contributions to my RRSPs. What I discovered was that by organizing my finances, I was able to reduce this type of stress and therefore leave myself with more energy to focus on the things that really mattered, like my creative pursuits.

So if money is a concern, then I would like offer a few ideas for you to think about as to how you can organize your finances and minimize this sort of stress in your life. Since each person's situation is unique, the solution that works best for you must be tailor-made to suit your needs. Obviously, I am not a licensed financial planner, nor am I pretending to be; however, here are five simple and practical things that worked for me that I can offer as a suggestion in order to alleviate some of the financial pressure that you might be experiencing:

- Track your expenses

  What this does is allow you to clearly see where your money goes and, as a result, can give you insight into which expenses have the potential to be minimized. It can also be a bit of a shock when you discover that you spend more money on shoes than you do on groceries.

- Create a monthly budget

  Obviously, this is a much easier task after you have tracked your expenses for a few months. Basically, this is where you decide how you want to spend your money so that you can minimize debt and maximize investment. It is also the point when you decide whether nutrition is more important than Louboutins.

Organization

- Make regular retirement contributions

    In terms of investments, one suggestion is to place a certain percentage of your monthly income into a retirement fund. So, if this is something that resonates with you then remember to factor this into your budget when you create it. Again, I would like to stress that I am not an investment banker so if this is something that is of interest to you, I suggest you do some research, meet with a registered financial planner and design a plan that will work best for you.

- Pay your taxes

    I once worked with a client who had not paid his taxes in eight years. His reasons were two-fold: a) taxes are annoying, and b) he was terrified that he owed a huge amount that he would never be able to pay back. So together, we managed to find an experienced accountant to help him file. In the end, and to his surprise, it balanced out so that he actually received a small refund. However, the greater reward for him was a newfound ability to sleep better at night, and you really couldn't attach a dollar amount to that.

- Reduce credit card debt

    When my brother passed away a few years ago, as the executor of the will, I found myself in the position of having to settle all of his accounts. The one thing that really stood out for me was that his credit card balance was so high that his minimum monthly payments barely made a dent on his card. He was indeed the ideal bank customer. Remember that finance companies want you to be in debt to them because that is how they make money. If you never paid interest on your lines of credit, loans, credit cards, and mortgages, the banking industry might potentially fail. A certain amount of debt is inevitable, so what are some strategies around it? One of the best ways is to pay off your credit card each month. Now since banks are counting on you not to be able to do this, as a result, they charge extremely high interest rates that can quickly lead to heavy debt loads. So if you already have accumulated an impossible amount to pay off in one go, do not lose hope, as my suggestion is that you apply for a line of credit at a lower interest rate to pay off the credit card, and then create a monthly payment plan to pay it off. This allows you to put the focus on making money as opposed to paying off debt. It's a minor but extremely powerful shift in mindset, and can help offer you a more secure sense of wellbeing.

Stand By Your Plan

As I mentioned earlier, lists are my *thing*, and the king of all lists for me is my to-do list. This one rules supreme. The one thing that I look forward to at the end of every workday is when I get to compose my to-do list for the next day. I attack these to-do lists with the kind of enthusiasm normally reserved for visits to the amusement park, or in some cases, the food court. My approach is simple: There are certain tasks that I must perform daily, so I write those down first. My next step is to transfer any of the activities I didn't complete on the present day's list, to the new one, in order of priority. Finally, I add any additional tasks that have cropped up.

Generally, my to-do list contains anywhere from one to twelve items, although I take so much joy in crossing items off these lists that I once went through a phase where I also included a detailed breakdown of mundane activities such as brushing my teeth, making coffee, and wiping the sink, just so I could strike them off the list with a gleeful black line. However, these days, I have learned to restrain myself and am much more concise. Occasionally, especially if the list is extra large, or I am feeling pressed for time, I will denote a time limit and timetable for each of the activities. This is often not necessary as I mainly refer to the daily timetable that I have designed for myself as my guide.

In addition to my daily planning, I also am a firm believer in one-year, five-year, and long-term (10–20 years) plans for my career path. Obviously, these plans are less detailed than my daily to-do lists, but they serve as guiding posts towards achieving my goals. These also serve as the basic framework for the daily to-do list, as they are how I decide where and how I am going to focus my daily energy in order to achieve my long-range plans.

The format I use for these is basic; at the top of the plan, I write down a numerical list of the goals I have for the upcoming year. From there, I break these large goals down into smaller achievable goals, and work out a tentative schedule in order to ensure that they happen. For example, here is a sample of one month from my one-year plan, from a number of years ago:

JULY

Admin:
        Adler Practicum Lab 1

Creative:
        Review/rehearse Flightmare
        Perform Fringe

Purposeful Jobs:
        Amazing Race Canada 5
        Coaching clients

Notice that I have divided my goals into three categories: Administrative, Creative, and Purposeful Jobs.

- Administrative Goals – I define these as administrative tasks that are directly related to achieving a career goal. These can include networking, contacting an important person, seminars, educational pursuits, organizing files, solving financial problems, etc.

- Creative Goals – These are the more exciting and larger reaching goals that generally the Administrative Goals support. For me, these are my creative writing projects, collaborations, performances, etc.—anything that I deem creative in nature.

- Purposeful Jobs – These are my present sources of income, and of course are the financial support for maintaining a secure lifestyle in order for me to achieve my creative goals. The term, *purposeful*, is consciously chosen, as not only do these positions provide financial solvency, but naming them as *purposeful* is also a mindset shift that helps me to not think of these jobs as merely a means to an end, but also as learning opportunities and/or potential networking prospects.

Another useful item, especially if you are self-employed or are planning on building your own business, is of course the business plan. I highly recommend that anyone who is self-employed or self generates finances should take the time to explore a comprehensive business plan. Not only does this help you to discover how and where to focus your energy, but it also will give you clear insight into whether or not there is a market for your business, and/or the viability of your proposed business. These days, thanks to our friend and occasional foe, the Internet, there are a number of resources that are readily available in order to research and formulate a business plan that best suits your needs.

The Twenty-Minute "Work-Out"

When it comes to effective planning, one of the most important elements is balance. I understand how difficult it is to juggle a full-time job, professional development, health concerns, and personal commitments, with building a business or working on creative projects. So I employ what I like to term the "twenty-minute rule", which is based on The Pomodoro Technique developed by Francesco Cirillo back in the 1980's. The reason behind this rule is simple and is based on my personal philosophy that a little bit of time spent on a project, on a daily basis, is better than no time spent on it at all. It also directly addresses the age-old procrastination proclamation of "if only I had the time." This is a comment that I all too often hear from my clients, which is a way of justifying their own lack of personal progress.

The way this works is simple. If you have a personal project that you want to do, and rather than be defeated because you can't set aside a full two hours in a day to attack it, because your schedule will not allow it, try this: Put your timer on for twenty minutes, and spend that twenty minutes each weekday working on said project. Mathematically, if you do this five days a week that equals one hour and forty minutes a week, or 6 hours and 40 minutes a month, or 86 hours and 40 minutes a year.

What it boils down to is that you can accomplish a lot in twenty minutes a day. Whole books can be written; in fact, the one you are reading right now was. So the next time you find yourself about to say, "If I only had the time," remember that if you spent twenty minutes a day, it is far more effective than the three-hour time slot you can never seem to find time for. Now that you have a better sense of how to organize your time, are you ready to jump in feet first and find out how you can use this newfound time to better your relationships? Add it to your schedule, and let's go.

Chapter Five

Relationships

Semper Fidelis

Back in 1965, Simon and Garfunkel recorded, "I Am a Rock," in my opinion one of the saddest songs ever written. It's right up there with Gilbert O'Sullivan's "Alone Again Naturally," and The Beatles' "Eleanor Rigby," which if you need a good cry, feel free to YouTube these boomer weepers. The ironic part is that all three songs were composed between 1965 and 1971, a period commonly known for its espousal of love and peace amongst the dawning of "The Age of Aquarius" and the afterglow of "The Summer of Love," whereas these particular tunes sound more like the soundtrack to "The Winter of Doom" and "The Age of Misery." In Simon and Garfunkel's piece, Paul Simon wails that he has built impenetrable fortress walls in order to protect himself from the difficulty of human interaction and a broken heart; after all, *"a rock feels no pain, and an island never cries."* The choice to eschew pain is a natural one, as no one really wants to experience hurt. However, the upside is that from deep pain comes huge opportunity for growth and the chance to experience the immense joy that comes from true personal connection. As Sandra Bernhard once said, "Without you, I'm nothing," and human beings definitely need community and interpersonal relationships in order to succeed.

The importance of relationships cannot be underestimated. Each and every one of us needs to be nurtured like a small pet, houseplant, or angelfish named "Bob," if you will. However, one of the hardest things every one of us has to do on a daily basis, be it in our personal lives or in our work environment, is negotiate our relationships with others. Since each experience can sometimes have long reaching effects, it is also imperative that you try and treat each person you meet with respect and kindness. This is an excellent practice, even if you think you are never going to see them again, because you can never be certain when your paths may cross.

I remember when I was a sixteen-year-old band geek, keen on Manhattan Transfer jazz pop medleys and John Phillip Sousa marches. During one rehearsal, my music teacher, Mr. Meyers, shared a story that had changed his life. Apparently, as a teenager, Mr. Meyers was one of the *cool* kids (unlike me); you know, the ones who the rest of us either revere or are terrified of. I fall into the latter category, as being a card-carrying clarinet player was not exactly the key to popularity. Mr. Meyers told us that when he was in high school, there was a guy, "Steve," whom Mr. Meyers liked to pick on... perhaps Steve too had an unhealthy obsession with Sousa marches? Mr. Meyers tortured Steve for a number of years, until they both graduated high school, moved on, and Mr. Meyers subsequently forgot about it.

Apparently, Steve did not. About fifteen years later, after Mr. Meyers had gone to music college, worked as a professional jazz musician, and graduated from teacher's college, he went for his first job interview as a teacher. Very nervous and anxious to get the job because he now had a family he needed to support, Mr. Meyers walked through the door into the principal's office, only to spot Steve, the guy he bullied from high school, sitting behind the principal's large desk. Mr. Meyers immediately felt quite small, and needless to say, he did not get the job. He did instead learn a very important lesson, and that is that you never know where someone is going to end up, so treat everyone you meet with respect, as if at any moment they could impact the outcome of your life.

To make his point abundantly clear, Mr. Meyers turned to Sara, one of the flute players, and indicating Clare, the oboist sitting next to her, said, "Sara, you better start kissing Clare's arse now, 'cause you never know when you might need her to hire you for a job." This story has stuck with me ever since, probably because Mr. Meyers was the only teacher I ever had who said "ass" in front of a large group of students. I think he was truly amazing.

A Yogi Bear Short of a Picnic

When it comes to seeking employment, I'm sure you have all heard that old adage, "It's not what you know, it's who you know." This is, of course, a total cliché, mainly because it is in fact completely true.

One summer, in between my second and third year of university, I auditioned for a nearby theme park and nabbed the lead role in the Woodland Theatre children's production of the enthusiastically titled, "Yogi Bear's Picnic." I was over the moon with my newfound stardom, until the reality of doing seven shows a day, six days a week, in a costume whose breathability was the equivalent of two double-ply garbage bags sealed in a lightweight shag rug, on an uncovered wooden stage that the sun heated up like an ad hoc barbeque, hit me like a discount bag of coal.

In addition to me losing sweat weight at an alarming rate, I also had to endure a seven-times-a-day attack of dozens of small children who, when invited to the stage, pounded on my costume like frustrated baby kangaroos. So with each and every foot-burning kick ball change I did, my desperation to escape grew stronger and stronger. This dissolution was only further reinforced when I overheard while in the bathroom of the green room, in hushed voices normally reserved for a church confessional or in a pricey shoe boutique, that I was in fact fifth choice for the part, as the four before me had wisely turned it down. I was distraught. How was I going to last all summer? I mean, this was only my second week.

So I did what any barely post teenage pre-adult does when they do not want to do something: I feigned illness. Lucky for me (or perhaps not so lucky), I already had a pre-existing condition that I could exploit, and I used it to back out of my contract. However, the problem was that I still needed a job because unemployment wasn't going to pay my university tuition, and apparently neither was my dad.

Fortunately, at my cast good-bye party (and yes, they still threw me a party because show biz types will look for any excuse to drink, even if it's because you've royally screwed them over), as I complained about my new dilemma, one of the actors mentioned that their neighbor, Annabella, worked as an assistant manager at a bank, and they needed tellers as soon as possible. So the next morning, with my head pounding with residual vodka, I pounded on Annabella's door. Two weeks later, I was a CSR at National Trust. The only reason I got the job is because even though Annabella didn't know me, she trusted her next-door neighbor and took his recommendation, even if he did dance in a children's show as an effeminate pink tiger.

The lesson here is that when it comes to business, any personal connection, no matter how tenuous, is better than no connection at all. Although interpersonal relationships enhance your life, it is also important, when either looking for new employment or building a client base for your own business, that you examine closely all your personal connections, and then from there look for ways to expand. As they say, we are all six degrees of separation from Kevin Bacon; and incidentally, I am only one, because I once met him on the street in Provincetown, although I didn't really notice him as I was far more taken by his wife, Kyra Sedgwick. Kevin seemed a little put off by that.

In most cases, there is very little that we can accomplish on our own, so it is a matter of figuring out how best to function in the world and work with others in the most effective manner possible. If you can manage to work this out, the rewards can be enormous.

What Gets in Your Way?

Generally, the element that stands in the way of healthy relationships, in pretty much every context, is negative, or "dark" emotions. For me, the light emotions include joy, love, adoration, contentment, etc., whereas the dark ones include anger and its close cousins—resentment, frustration, and jealousy—as well as fear and its companions: insecurity, anxiety, intimidation, etc. In my opinion, fear is actually the most difficult of the dark emotions to deal with, because it often informs or leads to other dark emotions, like anger and jealousy. In fact, I would argue that fear is at the base of most, if not all, human conflict, and is therefore the hardest obstacle we need to overcome if we want to form healthy relationships.

It's also very important to realize that you are not alone in this. Everyone around you also experiences a varying degree of fear in his or her day-to-day life. I myself am an anxious person by nature, and for years have parlayed this anxiety into motivational energy. People used to ask me, "Mark, how do you get so much done every day?" And I would answer, "I'm afraid; I'm very, very afraid."

What I've come to realize is that one of the keys of working with fear is to accept the fact that it exists, and that you are not going to be able to eliminate it completely. However, you can develop methods in which to cope with it. Be it spirituality, religion, meditation, or exercise, there are many avenues for you to explore and increase your level of self-awareness. The more self-aware you become, and the more you understand what triggers the dark emotions in you, especially what brings out the fear in you, the easier it will become to get along with others. After all, the more you can learn to forgive yourself, the easier it will become to forgive others, and this will naturally lead to stronger interpersonal relationships, and a more contented and integrated lifestyle.

Getting on With It

It's clear that positive relationships are not only important for an active and rewarding social life, but they also help enhance or facilitate your career. So how would you describe your interpersonal relationships, both at home, with your friends, and at work? How are they working for you? To what extent are you maximizing your contact list? If this is something that you want to improve or expand upon, then here are five suggested practical ways to help you, which have worked for me in the past.

1) Keep a Series of Contact Lists

For me, it all comes back to lists; and because I have three separate business streams, I have a contact list of colleagues that relates to each stream. I even suggest that you maintain a spreadsheet and log every person that you meet that may be important at some point to your business. In the chart, list their name, contact information, and how you met them, because these days, we are inundated with so much information that it is no longer sensible to rely simply on our memories alone. After all, I can barely remember what I ate for breakfast, let alone how I met "so and so," and "so and so" just might hold the key to the success of my next business idea.

Another suggestion is to keep a close eye all of your social contacts,

Relationships

because let's face it, you can never have too many friends. I can assure you that no one on their deathbed ever thinks, "Geez, I'm sad that I had such a good time with my friends; I wish I had worked harder instead." If it works for you, than I suggest you might want to even go so far as to write down, at the beginning of each week, those contacts you need to message socially in order to ensure that you maintain regular contact with everyone who is important to you. Remember, no one is ever going to accuse you of being too socially conscientious and/or too good of a friend.

2) Leverage Your Contact List

Now, there is, of course, no point in making a list unless you utilize it. So in addition to making sure you maintain your personal contacts, it also can be useful to periodically check in on your business contacts as well, especially if you rely on them as customers, clients, or for future contract work. It is important to remain professional, but also try to establish some kind of personal connection with them as well; as generally, people tend to like to either work with or hire their friends.

I have often heard people complain that no one makes the effort to keep in touch, and therefore, why should they? Well, the question I pose to you is, do you want to be part of the problem or part of the solution? So I highly recommend that you make the effort to consciously maintain connections, as eventually you will see it pay off.

This means that you must answer every email that is addressed to you personally, as nothing says, "I don't care about you" than an unanswered email or message. Yes, sometimes it is because you have a lot on your plate and it is hard to track everything. However, if you follow the steps outlined in the previous chapter about organization, this will naturally fall into place for you. This is extremely important because regardless of what is happening in your life, an unanswered message can be perceived as a passive-aggressive way of saying, "I don't want to engage." As a result, I make a concerted effort to answer every message personally addressed to me, because like I said, you never know when you might need support from someone else.

3) Ask for Help

On that note, all too often, people are too afraid to ask for help. This can be because they are shy, or concerned about being an imposition, or worried that they may be judged. If you are afraid to ask because you do not want to appear vulnerable, then I encourage you to consider how the expression of vulnerability can lead to true connection with others. After all, when it comes down to it, what is inevitable in all our lives beyond death and taxes? Fear. I have it. You have it. The parking meter guy has it. So does everyone else. So the next time you are feeling socially anxious at a cocktail party or networking event, slowly inching towards the exit, wishing that you had stayed at home with Netflix and a bag of chips, remember that everyone else in the room is probably just as frightened as you are. It is actually the one thing you have in common with everyone, although you might not want to use it as your opening line. Believe me, I know. Once, at a party, I decided to experiment with this introduction: "Hi, I'm Mark, and I am really, really scared—how are you?" The result? I was home by nine, watching reruns of "The Love Boat" on YouTube. So save that type of reveal for after you have established a connection, but if asking for help is something that worries you, try and uncover what the source is of your mindset regarding receiving help from others. What did you learn as a child about asking for help? How did your parents, friends, or teachers greet your requests for help? How do you feel this has affected the way you ask for help in your present life?

If you discover that you are indeed afraid to ask for help, then I invite you to look at it from an alternate perspective. I know that when someone appeals to me for help and/or support, either as a friend, consultant, or mentor, I view it as a compliment. In my opinion, being asked for help is a personal validation, as it means that whoever is asking believes in what I have to offer. It's a wonderful feeling.

It is not a sign of weakness to ask for assistance, as very few projects were ever completed in a vacuum. The truth is that humans are pack animals and therefore often rely on community. Help is at your disposal more than you realize, so why not make the most of it?

4) Avoid Negativity

Unfortunately, there are people out there who, because of their own fears and insecurities, want to drag you down, because when people are unhappy in their lives, they want others to experience their unhappiness as well. Hence, the expression, *misery loves company*. It's a common occurrence, and one you may have to face quite regularly. One thing that's helped me in the past is the realization that there are essentially four ways human beings relate to themselves and their world:

- I'm okay, you're okay – These people are the happy, kind ones. (NB: I am not naturally one of these of people… but I aspire to be.)

- I'm okay, you're not okay – These people tend to be the judgmental ones that tend to blame others and the world for their problems.

- I'm not okay, you're okay – These are the ones who beat themselves up when things go wrong, tend to suffer lowered self-esteem, take the blame first, and are quite often people pleasers who put others needs before their own.

And finally ...

- I'm not okay, you're not okay – These are the individuals who really struggle with their interpersonal relationships.

It's important to note that no one is one particular type only, as we can flow through these states of relating, depending on the situation and how we are feeling. It is, however, useful to identify which mindset most informs your primary relationship to yourself and the world, as well as to identify the relationships in your life that need the most work and attention.

This type of self-examination can be scary, as it means you may need to let go of your own misperceptions, and/or relationships that are in essence offering more pain than joy. However, if you are willing to make the effort to examine all your relationships, the reward in the end will be well worth the effort.

5) Never Under Estimate the Power of Kindness

If you find that you are struggling with many interpersonal relationships in your life, I strongly recommend reading *The Four Agreements: A Practical Guide to Personal Freedom*, by Don Miguel Ruiz. Essentially, it boils down to the following:

- Be impeccable with your word – "The first rule of 'Fight Club' is you don't talk about 'Fight Club.'" So here's the thing: If you can learn not to say anything mean or gossipy about anyone ever, then no one can ever be upset at you for saying something about them. On top of that, it also means that people will realize that since you do not gossip about others, you most likely will not gossip about them either, and therefore they will trust you more. So by avoiding negative talk about others, you are actually promoting better relationships with other people. In conjunction, you are also decreasing drama and stress, and increasing contentment and good will. So the next time you're standing at the water cooler, and you feel tempted to gossip about how your colleague, "Miriam," doesn't do anything all day because she's busy posting Sneezing Panda videos on Facebook, think about the long term effects of what you choose to say, and whether they will bring happiness to your life or open the door to negativity and anxiety.

- Free yourself from taking anything personally – It happens all the time; you're walking into a mall, and the guy in front of you not only doesn't hold the door for you, but he also shoots you a nasty look as if your very presence on the planet is somehow a personal affront to him. This person is a complete stranger, so therefore you haven't done anything to them, but yet you still feel offended and/or hurt by their behavior. So what happens if you let it go and realize that the way they are acting has absolutely nothing to do with you, and thus there is no need to take it personally? Moreover, what happens if you take this concept and apply it to all of your interpersonal relationships? If you're already being impeccable with your word, then you've already reduced the likelihood of offending anyone; so therefore, if someone is acting out in front of you, then chances are it has nothing to do with you. Can you picture what your life would be like if you removed this type of drama from it? How much more free time would you have to do what you really want to do? And how much happier would you be overall? Just imagine the freedom.

- Free yourself from making assumptions – How many times have you caught yourself thinking something to the effect of, "Well, I know that they're thinking this, that, and the other thing about me." But do you? How much do you really know about what other people are thinking? How much do you create stories that prop up your inherent beliefs about yourself? More importantly, how would you feel if you let go of these assumptions about others and their opinions? Just imagine how much brain space you would have for other thoughts and potential creative projects. Remember, your life is what you create, and what you create is strongly dependent on what you choose to perceive. So maybe it's time for you to make some new choices.

- Always do your best – Remember, no one is perfect; so try your hardest and be kind to yourself whenever you make a mistake or slip. It is only by learning to forgive yourself that you can learn to forgive others.

These are just a few suggestions of actions you can take in order to maintain strong relationships with others, as well as develop new healthy and productive ones. The important thing is to remember that few can succeed alone; there's a reason that phrases such as "it takes a village" are popular. So when looking forward at your goals and how to achieve them, consider carefully what kind of help you need to do so. Consider carefully how you can strengthen your relationships so that you are fully supported on your journey towards success. Kindness is key; so let's dive a little deeper into how this type of generosity can positively impact your life.

Chapter Six

Generosity

Pilots, Chocolates, and Christmas Candles

When I was in grade seven, I was obsessed with being the top chocolate-almond and Christmas-candle seller. My school was raising money for charity, and I saw it as an opportunity to increase my social profile, because I was the kind of nerdy kid who thought that being a top peddler of waxy sugar and warped wax candles would somehow make me more popular. I failed on both accounts. Not only were my efforts to sell second rate, but being number forty-six on the list of fundraisers didn't exactly help my social life either. However, hawking my wares around 1970s suburbia did teach me a thing or two about generosity—mainly that a ninety pound, blue-eyed, blonde thirteen-year-old, who looks about nine, stands a good chance at manipulating money out of people's pockets. Unfortunately, just not enough to compete with those kids whose father is the CEO of a large corporation and forced their employees to buy their kid's candy.

When you think about the concept of generosity, how often do you think it is about giving money or gifts as opposed to the concept of just giving? For example, a co-worker buys donuts for everyone, and you immediately think, "Wow, aren't they generous?" And/or, "How long do I have to ride the elliptical to make up for this mango macaroon donut?" However, generosity is not just limited to money or gifts. Generosity comes in many forms, and even encompasses creativity.

Forgive or Forget It

Back in the mid-2000s, when I trained at the Canadian Film Centre as a screenwriter, one of our many tasks was to come up with three original ideas for a television series, and then pitch our ideas to the group. For those of you unfamiliar with this concept, in its simplest terms, it is a nerve-racking process in which stammering red-faced individuals stand up and risk humiliation by describing their ideas for a television show, to large groups of people who then proceed to rip it to shreds. In effect, it is a creative colonoscopy sans sedation.

In the end, my favorite one, entitled *Fashion Victim*, was selected as the one I should develop. So after six rather painful hair-pulling weeks, I came up with a twenty-two minute pilot about a neurotic feminist producer who is forced to deal with a crazy cast of characters, including her boss—a pompous, sexist, self-involved male executive—who threatens both her failing career and her sanity. Now if this idea sounds strangely familiar to you, then chances are that you are a fan of *30 Rock*, because that was essentially what I created (#somuchfororiginality). For the trailer that I produced, I even cast a mid-30s actress, with medium brown hair and the same pair of glasses that Tina Fey wears.

I have always believed that we are all connected by the collective unconscious, and that creative ideas are just out there floating in the ether. Once you put an idea out there into the universe, if you love it, act quick, because if you don't, chances are that someone else will. For example, *30 Rock* debuted in September 2006, which means it was probably pitched in 2005, and developed as a pilot in early 2006, and therefore developed around the exact time I was working on mine. So either Tina Fey took my idea or I stole hers. It's impossible to say, but let's just hope I steal another one that will make me as rich as she is, so I don't end up having to steal from her actual bank account.

Generosity

In the book, *It's Not How Good You Are, It's How Good You Want To Be*, ex-advertising executive, Paul Arden, expounds on the idea that you should not "covet your ideas." Arden explains that many people are secretive at work because they are afraid that their ideas will be stolen, and they will not get the credit they feel they deserve. The problem, Arden states, is that chronic hoarding of creativity can lead to living off your reserves and the risk of having your ideas become stale. Arden asserts that one should always give away everything they know, and that even more will come back to them—a sort of a creative karma, if you will. There is no shortage of creativity in the world, as there is a constant network of ideas available; therefore, our job is simply to figure out a way to tune into them. In addition, since you are a unique individual with your own individual point of view, then if your idea is similar to others, it can never be exactly the same.

I find this concept incredibly liberating but how does it resonate with you? Are you the type to share your ideas? Or do you like keeping them to yourself out of fear they might get stolen? I would strongly encourage you to experiment with sharing your ideas and see what happens. After all, as they say, "What goes around comes around," and therefore, if you share your ideas, then more than likely others will share with you, and suddenly you may have even more to choose from. If you think back to the notion of relationships, in which very few can succeed alone, a similar principle applies; and therefore being generous with your creativity may potentially pay off more than you realize.

The Forgiveness Follies

What about generosity of spirit? How does that play into your life? How willing are you to forgive? Or do you hang onto resentments and grudges like Reese Witherspoon's character in *Big Little Lies*, and "nurture them like small pets?" If this is something that you do, then how does this serve you? What is the effect of holding onto your anger towards others? What would happen if you let go of your rage; how would you feel then? How much room would there be for possibility and growth?

Years ago, during a difficult part of my life when I was feeling particularly creatively uninspired, I tried an experiment. I challenged myself to read twelve different self-help books, and to blog about each chapter in each book, at least two to three times a week, with the premise of "how will my life change in one year?" as my guide. To tell you the truth, my life changed very little. However, I did gain a much broader perspective of myself, and a larger sense of my relationship with the world. It also allowed me to read a wide range of books on the topic of self-improvement, some that were incredibly helpful.

One of the books that stuck with me is Louise Hay's, *I Can Do It – How to use Affirmations to Change Your Life,* and to this day, I still consciously practice many of the affirmations she shares. The one section that really stands out for me is Hay's chapter on Forgiveness, in which she likens holding onto your past to a self-imposed emotional prison. Hay states that we need to take responsibility for our own thoughts and feelings in order to learn to master our ability to respond to them. After all, by not doing this, we prevent ourselves from enjoying the present moment.

In this particular chapter, Hay offers the affirmation of, *"It is only by forgiving yourself that you can forgive others."* This highlights two different things for me: First, if you are hard on others, then chances are you are probably even harder on yourself. Secondly, if you could be gentler with yourself, just imagine how much easier it would be to project that same kindness onto others. It is important to recognize that you can only control your own reactions and responses, so therefore you must let go of how others react, and try to take care of yourself.

Generosity

In essence, by being kind and generous to yourself, it opens you up to being kinder to those around you. This generosity of spirit can also be applied to how you choose to serve others. It could potentially mean that you want to make volunteering a bigger part of your life, or you want to spend more time focused on the needs of others. Regardless of what you do with this, it will change how you choose to respond to others, and how much more generous you are able to be with others with your time.

On the topic of time, I am not ashamed to admit that I have clocked my fair share of hours in therapy. Basically, I have been in and out of therapy for over twenty-five years, and have gone through more therapists in my lifetime than pairs of winter boots. Every therapist has offered their own unique insights into my experiences and character; however, the one common thought that links all my therapeutic experiences, is the phrase, "*Mark, you are incredibly hard on yourself.*" It is clear that a large part of my self-journey is to figure out ways in order to be kinder to myself. It's not easy, as the default mechanisms that are wired into my nervous system generally fall under the category of negative self-talk. Even in the most innocuous of situations, my industrious brain will figure out a way to torture me. For example, I might be in the dry goods aisle of the grocery store, reach for a box of instant mac'n'cheese, and my inner voice will suddenly screech at the top of its lungs, "What are you doing? You can't eat that garbage; it has no nutritional value. Who do you think you are? Are you twelve years old?" and so forth, until I place the box guiltily back on the shelf, furtively looking over my shoulder to see if anyone has witnessed my near culinary crime.

Unfortunately, I have the type of brain that does not know when to take a hike, even when I'm in the wilderness literally taking a hike. There was one Thanksgiving where my friends and I rented a cottage out in the country for the weekend. On the Sunday afternoon, I decided to relax on the couch. After all, this was the first time in a long time that I did not have to be anywhere, and there was nothing I had to accomplish. It was one of those rare moments of pure unfettered downtime. So there I am, lying there in a near state of Zen, for almost... twenty-two seconds when suddenly out of the blue, my brain hurls me back to the time at the end of my first year at theatre school. As part of the school's Spring Showcase, a large portion of first-year students were thrown together to perform a chorus number from "Will Roger's Follies." For those of you unfamiliar with the show, let's just say the number we did was performed sitting on a long row of chairs, and was comprised of an intricate set of complicated interactive arm and leg choreography. Unfortunately for me, I have always had a tenuous hold on hand-eye coordination, and within the first eight bars, I was one beat behind.

Since there were twenty-five of us on stage, it took a while for the audience to notice, but as the number progressed, what began as a few isolated snickers, rose to heckling rows of laughter as I blissfully and obliviously pummeled the choreography. It was not until after the show that I discovered my folly. Needless to say, when I realized I had been one beat behind for the entire number, my stomach plunged to my ankles, and my ears flushed a deep scarlet. My embarrassment was only re-enforced when I was handed a tape of my performance for posterity. My only saving grace in all of this is that mercifully VHS tape disintegrates, and very few people still have a VHS player in order to witness my deep choreographic shame.

However, the important learning here is why, when I was relaxing, did my mind choose to go there? It is obvious that somewhere along the line, I was given the message that I was not allowed to relax, that I always had to be on guard, and now my hyper vigilant brain chronically looks for ways to re-enforce this core belief, at my psychological expense.

Generosity

It's important to realize that generosity is not necessarily limited to an outward motion, as it is also something that we need to offer to ourselves. In order to best serve others and to be at your best, you need to be kind to yourself. This means taking care of your mind, body, and spirit I have had to consciously figure out ways to help me be kinder to myself. As a result, here is a list of some of the things I have done, which may or may not be helpful for you, to become more generous with yourself. For simplicity sake, I have divided them into three categories: mind, body, and spirit.

Self-Generosity Hints

Body:

- Eat healthy – Yes, I realize this is completely obvious, but clearly the benefits of this are enormous, or else it would not have been written and harped on ad nauseum. This is something I really struggle with because not only are onion rings my favorite food group, but I really do not enjoy cooking. So my best option is to try and coerce as many people as I can to cook for me—that, and to try and date Europeans because their mothers always want to cook for you.

- Exercise regularly – Again, this is truly important, as not only does it help alleviate stress, but the endorphins make you feel good as well. It also helps you to feel better about yourself and increase your self-confidence. Personally, I try to work out five times a week, because a) Admittedly, I'm super vain, and b) I'm super anxious, so it helps to keep me from going ballistic in the grocery store line-up. Although I did completely lose it post–workout the other day, with a woman who was embroiled in a ten-minute debate with the cashier over the price of a $1.97 toothbrush. I told her that I would give her two dollars just to leave the store. Clearly an extra twenty minutes on the elliptical machine that day would have benefited me. However, I did manage to offer myself a generosity of spirit and forgave myself for this misstep.

- Get enough sleep – How many of you suffer from FOMO? How many of you do not know what FOMO is? It is, as the youth say, the "fear of missing out." This has been a prominent fear in my life ever since my dad said to me when I was fourteen, "Mark, don't ever turn down an invitation, 'cause they will never ever invite you again." So for the next thirty-five odd years, I ran myself ragged trying to be six places at once. What this led to was exhaustion and a bi-monthly two to three-day breakdown where I would turn off my phone, my computer, and hide from the world. So take it from me; figure out how much sleep you need daily, and try and commit to it. You will be shocked by how much better you can handle everything else.

- Take deep breaths – Yes, breathing is an automatic mechanism that your body does. However, I discovered that I quite often hold my breath for long periods of time. This becomes quite obvious when you work in a cubicle environment and your neighbors complain to you about your chronic cryptic sighing. So do your co-workers a favor: Pay attention to your breathing patterns, and notice if you have a tendency to hold your breath. Consciously inhale deeply, and notice how this makes you feel. When you're faced with a stressful situation, try to allow yourself to breathe even deeper; it truly is one of the easiest and kindest things you can do for yourself.

- Enjoy moderation – Okay, I am the type of person who never takes sips. In fact, when presented with a glass of anything, I will generally finish it in about fifteen seconds. I guess it's because I am a "completionist," and I just want to get the job done. However, you can imagine the impact this has when you are hanging out with friends at the office holiday party. I have been that guy, who drops his phone in the toilet after a rather loud impromptu performance of "I Wanna Dance With Somebody," at the company karaoke party. So I understand the importance of moderation, as it is something I have to work at consciously to achieve. I believe that since apparently everything causes cancer, you should not have to deprive yourself. However, enjoy what you want but don't go overboard, as long as you're not hurting anyone else or yourself.

- Rest when you're sick – This seems simple, but it's not. If you're like me, then you take great pride in your work. It may even be a large part of how you identify as a person. Therefore, it is important that you keep the ball rolling regardless of how you might be feeling. So even when you're sick, you might find yourself sitting at your desk, sneezing, sniffling, and spreading your germs liberally around like a drunken crop duster. Believe me, no one wants you around when you're like that. So next time you're unwell, stay home and rest; it might just be the kindest thing you could do for yourself and all of your work mates.

- See a doctor regularly – When was the last time you had a physical? As someone with a number of chronic autoimmune disorders, I cannot stress enough the importance of seeing a doctor regularly. After all, you have one body, one life, and the responsibility to take the best care of it that you can.

- Get your teeth cleaned – You ever have one of those dreams where all your teeth fall out? I do, on a fairly regular basis. According to one dream analyst, it means that you regret something you said, because just like the teeth, words have fallen out of your mouth that cannot be put back in. Well, I know that sometimes I struggle to control what comes out of my mouth, but I can control my dental care. This is coming from someone who dreads brushing their teeth every morning. I really can't stand it—the whole drooling messy mouth, the spitting, the mess it makes in your sink. Nonetheless, I get my teeth cleaned every three to four months, and also every morning on top of brushing, I floss, rubber tip, and sulca brush, which if you don't know what that is, look it up—it is an absolute must for those of you who, like me, eat a cracker and get instant tartar build-up. Honestly, taking care of your teeth is something that is invaluable as you get older. Remember, if you want to take a bite out of life or dig your teeth into something, then wouldn't it be better if you have something you can actually do that with.

- Get your blood tested for vitamin deficiencies – I am affected by Crohn's Disease, which is an inflammatory bowel illness that affects how well I digest food and absorb nutrients. Therefore, as part of my yearly physical, I get regular blood tests to monitor my vitamin and mineral levels; in particular, B12, D, calcium, and iron. I feel this is an important practice because if there is a problem, I can attend to it quickly before it becomes a larger problem. I recommend that you speak to your doctor about checking your vitamin levels, particularly if you suffer from chronic low energy. It might not be that you are simply lazy and addicted to Netflix, as much as there may be an easily solved medical reason that has you glued to the couch.

- Be an advocate for your own health – As a person who has been to proverbial hell and back with my own health, I know for a fact that this is incredibly important, and it is an extremely generous gift you can give to yourself. It simply means that you need to take an active role in your own medical care. Only you know your body and what feels right and what doesn't. It also means you will be unpopular with medical staff, and more than likely labeled a "bad" patient. However, "bad" patients usually fare much better and get well quicker than their compliant "good" patients. My recommendation is not to rely on the Internet for information but to go directly to the source. Ask the doctors to explain themselves, ask difficult questions, and voice your concerns. If you had to have a major appliance or vehicle serviced, wouldn't you want to know where your money is going? The same goes for your body; you only have one, so why not get the best service you can get for yourself. Believe me, I know that you're worth it.

Mind:

- Stimulation – Every morning while my dad sipped his instant coffee, he would do a Sudoku. This, I could never understand because, to me, doing these types of puzzles for entertainment is akin to spending a riveting Saturday night scrubbing the toilet bowl with a Q-tip; that is, a lot of work, pain, and suffering with very little reward. However, Dad claimed that it helped keep his mind active, which at his age was necessary; although I would argue that you must keep your mind active and stimulated at any age. So whether it's the dreaded Sudoku, crocheting, or simply reading a book, I strongly suggest that you integrate mind-activating activities into your regular routine. It's truly a kind and generous thing you can do for your own psyche.

- Life Learning – One of the most important concepts that I discovered during my training as a professional coach, is the difference between the "judger" and the "learner" mindsets. When you activate the "judger" part of your brain, you make assumptions, and it can often close down your willingness to be open. However, when you shift focus and engage your "learner" mindset, it ignites your curiosity and a corresponding open mindedness. You can argue that the "judger" mindset is necessary to make decisions and to discern what is or is not important, and I would agree that you definitely need to know when and how to use it. However, when it comes to how you approach the world, what would happen if you allowed yourself to be curious about a problem, as opposed to angry or defensive? What if education was much more than organized or formal, and you were able to make yourself a proverbial *student of life*? There is a reason that the cliché, "Well, you learn something new every day," exists, as it is the credo of the life- long learner. How would it feel if that was your approach? How more exciting would life be? And what would you gain from it? This type of curiosity is a form of generosity that you not only can offer to yourself, but it is also a gift you can give to others.

- Relaxation – How often do you allow yourself to truly relax? This does not mean drinking a martini while doing your taxes or vacuuming, but honestly just relaxing. When you are young, you are very in tune with the concept of having fun. However, as you age, and your responsibilities in life increase, quite often the amount of fun can conversely decrease. So how much fun do you allow yourself to have on a regular basis? What do you do for fun? And how can you increase the amount of fun (within reason) in your life? It's different for each person, but it's definitely an area worth exploring.

- Meditation and Mindfulness – This seems to be all the rage these days. I even know of people within the corporate sector offering mindfulness courses as part of their weekly interactions with their respective teams. There is a ton of information out there about meditation and mindfulness, so I will not embark on a huge discourse about it. However, let me say this: There is not a single self-help guru out there that does not practice meditation, and I suggest that it is a necessary part of finding balance within your life. So be kind to yourself; look into it, and start slow— even two or three minutes a day can have huge benefits to your levels of concentration and ability to handle stress. My only suggestion is that you practice when sitting, because if you try it lying down, you'll be asleep in seconds. I know this firsthand all too well.

- Therapy – I am the type of person who continually wants to gain a deeper understanding of how I relate to the world; and I strategize ways in order to not only find balance but to overcome the constant and cyclical obstacles that stand in my way. As a side effect of my efforts, I have also gained deeper understanding into how humans relate to each other and what makes them tick. This in turn has heightened my ability to be empathic and to show compassion towards others. When you make the effort to really understand yourself and what triggers you, it helps you to minimize the amount of unrecognized pain you may be experiencing in your life. It also leads to a greater compassion towards yourself and the rest of the human race. It truly is one of the kindest things you can do for yourself.

Spirit:

- Compliment Lists – My whole life I have struggled with feelings of lowered self-esteem and it has been extremely easy for me to focus on the negative, especially having worked continually in a field where you are constantly being scrutinized and offered "notes," which is a relatively innocuous word for "now we're going to destroy you and you'd better fix it." So in order to combat this continual assault of negativity, years ago, I got in the practice of writing down every professional compliment I have ever received, so when I am feeling battered to the ground, I can look and see concrete proof of my success and abilities. So I strongly suggest that if you suffer from similiar feelings that you start to track the positive re-enforcement that you receive, for not only will it give you concrete proof of your strengths, but it also helps shift your mindset from the negative to the positive, in a very real way.

- Balance – Life is a constant juggling act. It doesn't matter whether you're in a relationship, have a high profile career, have children, or are a single unemployed artist type—it is all about achieving and maintaining equilibrium. This is not easy, and chances are you will have to spend your entire life trying to accomplish this. The important thing is to realize that you are not alone; everyone is going through the same thing. The only thing I can suggest is an awareness of this need, and a gentleness of spirit as you move towards it.

- Self-Forgiveness – One of the most revelatory things I have ever encountered are the affirmations from Louise Hay's *Heal Your Life*, around the concept of forgiveness. There are three of them, which I recite on a daily basis:

  - I give myself the gift of freedom from the past, and move with joy into the now.

  - As I forgive myself, it becomes easier to forgive others.

  - I forgive myself for not being perfect; I am living the very best way I know how.

I was brought up with the idea that forgiving others was a great kindness, but these affirmations are even more important because they help me to remember to be kind and compassionate with myself as well. This in turn helps me to be even more kind towards others, and is perhaps one of the greatest gifts you can give to yourself. This is a kindness that you truly deserve, so why not start today? After all, what do you have to lose?

Generosity comes in many forms, but it always starts at home. It's time for you to open your doors and arms to your own self-healing. This can take a little imagination, so let's now explore what role this plays in your life, and how you can maximize its potential.

Chapter Seven

Imagination

"Come with me and you'll be... in a world of pure imagination."
– Willy Wonka, Charlie and the Chocolate Factory

The Wonkatania

One of my favorite times of the year as a child was Easter, not because of the sugar-fuelled marshmallow candy Easter egg hunts, but purely because it meant that *Willy Wonka and the Chocolate Factory* was on television. This was long before iTunes or Netflix, and even before the long gone beige pants/denim shirt wonder of Blockbuster Video had entered the scene—you were at the mercy of TV programming, and event television was a real thing. They played it every spring, and even though I was in equal parts completely fascinated and horrified by Veruca Salt's greedy lust for geese that laid golden eggs, and Violet Beauregard's gum smacking pride and blueberry juice comedown, what I was most enraptured by was Charlie Bucket's epic rise to glory.

I identified very much with Charlie, not only because he was given an unfortunate surname, just like me (after all, with a last name like Peacock, you either need to be exceedingly resilient or extremely well off to pay for therapy, if you wanted to survive the scars of schoolyard taunts), but I also identified with the character, because like Charlie, I understood what it felt like to have my

Forgive or Forget It

guardian be unable to get out of bed. Only unlike Charlie, the reasons behind my mother being bedridden were more psychological than physical like his grandparents. Finally, and of course most importantly, the biggest similarity between Charlie and me was our mutual fondness for navy blue turtlenecks and 70s side parts.

However, I think the thing that I identified with the most was the fact that like Charlie, I considered myself to be an underdog. I still do. Nevertheless, in the magical world drawn from Roald Dahl's rather bleak imagination, I could join Charlie and go along for a psychedelic ride on the *Wonkatania*, be gob smacked by an *Everlasting Gobstopper*, and break the literal glass ceiling in an elevator. Yes, Charlie Bucket was my type of hero, and the basis of my belief that even though I did not have a lot, things could get better, especially if I used my imagination.

And so I did.

When my mom left my dad and me when I was thirteen, my dad's reaction was to go out every night to the Racquet Ball Club, to amuse, schmooze, and booze his sorrows away. I, on the other hand, employed a different strategy: I dyed my white-blonde hair green with food coloring, smoked menthol cigarettes in the garage, and lip-synced The B-52's "Rock Lobster" while I danced it out on top of Dad's octagonal Colonial-inspired coffee table from Leon's. I'm sure he would have been "thrilled" had he known. The fear of getting caught did not deter me, because I believed that rock stars destroyed hotel rooms, and definitely did not need their mothers.

When my first girlfriend dumped me at sixteen, I created an imaginary persona, "Kevin," who was much more handsome than me, a better dresser with a cooler haircut, and actually capable of catching a football. "Kevin" exuded the kind of confidence that in turn got him all the girls, and the admiration of all the guys. I remember I used to walk through the mall, engulfed deep in the fantasy that I

Imagination

(aka Kevin) was turning heads, and everyone I encountered either wanted to know me or be me. I can only imagine how I appeared to others when they saw an impossibly diminutive skinny blonde teenager, who looked about twelve, swinging from clothing rack to clothing rack through Simpson Sears, like he was king of the retail jungle.

When I was in third year in the music program at university, I had a major operation in which they removed a foot and a half of my small intestine, which forced me into the ICU, and subjected my battered body to six weeks in a hospital bed. So in order to pass the long hours, I would listen to a cassette tape of an orchestral version of Stravinsky's ballet, Petroushka, and imagine I was the first chair clarinetist. Did I mention that I was a life-long band geek? In all of these cases, my imagination served as my primary method of emotional survival and hope.

I am certain that as a child, you too, daily if not hourly, accessed your imagination in order to either pass the time or protect yourself from events that you did not quite understand, or that perhaps even frightened you. It is unfortunate that as you mature, you are quite often given less and less opportunity to exercise your imagination, particularly in such a laissez-fair way. As adults, the focus often shifts to the practical and logical, and the inner creativity that you possess is suppressed in order to conform to societal expectations. It's possible that you may have even had an experience, or even several, in which you were actively discouraged or shamed when you continued to exercise your imagination. The good news is that it has not left you, and it never will. For as long as you are alive, it is an intrinsic part of your makeup as a human being. The question is, how do you continue to engage with it, and how can you make it work to your advantage?

A good place to start is to ruminate on how you used your imagination in the past? How did it help you? What fantasies did you enjoy? What were some of your go-to things to imagine? What were some of your favorite games to play as a child? What kind of songs did you make up? What kind of roles did you like to play? How many of these have you taught to your own children, or perhaps even still, secretly or not so secretly, like to play? Your imagination is a powerful tool that is always at your disposal, but the question is, how readily accessible is it to you? And how big of a role does it play in your life these days? In what ways do you now use your imagination?

Years ago, I took a six-week night class in Art Therapy. At the beginning of each of the classes, the facilitator allowed us a half hour to sit and draw or paint whatever we wanted, using a variety of mediums. It was an exercise without parameters, and without judgment or critique at the end. It was simply something that we could do for ourselves for the purpose of self-exploration. I found this to be incredibly cathartic because, as a child, I had a rather strained relationship with the visual arts. There are two reasons behind this. First of all, my parents unconsciously streamlined each of us three kids into different categories: my brother was the athlete, my sister was the visual artist, and I was the "musician," and we were not encouraged, nor did we rarely stray out of our lanes, even though we each had a modicum of ability in every area. Secondly, when I was in grade four, I remember I received my report card, and although I had A's and B's in every subject, in Art I was given a D. When I asked my mother about this, she told me that my teacher, Mrs. Cormier, had told her that she thought I had "no talent."

No talent.

Imagine telling a nine-year-old that they have no talent. Since I was a sensitive child, I was incredibly disheartened by this comment, and as a result, from then on, I made very little effort in visual arts. I also no longer felt guilty for having laughed my head off at Mrs. Cormier when she was standing on the desk with the Advent

Wreath on it, to hang something above the blackboard, and she slipped and landed arse-first in the middle of the wreath, with her bellbottoms and platform shoes dangling over the fir branches.

So you can imagine my discomfort when, after six weeks of our impromptu "anything goes" art sessions at the Art Therapy course, we were suddenly asked to present our work. When I finally got up the guts to show mine, I was flabbergasted when one of my classmates raised their hand and asked me which art school I had attended. Although I am not by any stretch an amazing visual artist, it was in that moment that I realized that our inner critic, and the lessons (and sometimes traumas) we encounter as children, can often get in the way of our creativity and allowing us to use our imagination.

So what kind of creative traumas have you experienced? If so, how have they affected your relationship with your imagination? How do they affect you now?

Exercise: Adventure Time

There are many ways we express our imagination as children, be it through the visual arts (painting/finger painting/coloring/crafting, etc.), music, writing, or play acting, or even more simply, most of us as children have incorporated imagination into our everyday play and games. I would now like to invite you to choose one (or more than one if you are inspired) of the following, and set aside thirty minutes of personal time to explore it.

- Writing: journaling/creative writing/short stories/poetry/song lyrics

- Visual Arts: painting/coloring/crafting/sewing/finger painting

- Music: singing, playing an instrument, listening to recordings

- Play: play acting, lip syncing, day dreaming

Please note that if none of the above resonate with you, feel free to choose something that is intrinsically important to you. Remember, the point of this exercise is not to be "good" at the activity but to allow yourself to access your inner child, and to explore with that same innocence and abandon that you had as a child. Essentially, allow yourself the freedom to literally play in the moment.

Set your timer and go.

Exercise Debrief:

How was that experience for you? How did it feel? What did you discover about yourself? Take a moment and reflect on what came up for you during the process?

Now let's apply these methods in a more practical way. How do you feel that imagination plays into helping you achieve your goals? How do you feel that the great artists, scientists, financiers, entrepreneurs, and visionaries in the past used their imaginations? What does our imagination offer as a way of moving forward in our lives?

I would like to now invite you to try one or all three of these writing exercises to help apply your imagination to your own life. If writing is not the best way for you to enjoy these exercises, than it is just as effective to express it in the way you are most comfortable.

- The Perfect Day:

  Imagine the ultimate day in your future. What are you doing? Where are you? What is going through your mind? How do you

Imagination

feel? How do others react to you? What does the next day look like?

- The Acceptance Speech

  Imagine you have just won an award for your chosen area of expertise, and the whole world is watching. The announcer calls your name… what happens next? How do you react? What do you say when you reach the podium? Who do you thank? What is it that you want to say to the world? Who are you being in this moment? Who do you want the world to see you as?

- The Ultimate Introduction

  Imagine you are about to receive a lifetime achievement award for your life's work. Write out that introduction from the point of view of the person who is giving it. How do they see you? How do you want to be seen? What have you accomplished? Imagine the audience reaction. How do you want them to feel? How do you want to be acknowledged? And what do you ultimately want to be recognized for? For an added bonus, imagine who would be the ultimate person to give that introduction. Afterwards, read it out loud, and think about how you would feel if you were in the audience and heard that speech.

Keep in mind that these exercises are designed to help you access your imagination, so it does not matter if it is real at the moment or even likely based on your present path. Remember, life is choices, and things can and will change. So if you want to imagine you're winning an Oscar, even though you work in the medical field, that is perfectly fine. The point of these exercises is not only to flex the imagination muscle but also to help you to continue to illuminate your core values.

Our core values are what consciously and unconsciously guide us. Whether we are aware of them or not, these principles inform our decisions, both big and small. When your core values are in line with your path, you feel a sense of peace and purpose. So using your imagination can help identify what is important to you and what it is you want to achieve. Einstein said it best, "Imagination is everything. It is the preview of life's coming attractions." And everyone knows how that turned out for him. Furthermore, by accessing your imagination, you can begin to explore what is possible, as you can only make something possible if you can see it. Visualization is an incredibly powerful skill, so let's explore how you can incorporate it into your life and make the most of it.

Chapter Eight

Visualization

You Love Me; You Really, Really Love Me

Nearly 30 million viewers watched the Academy Awards in 2019, as this is one of the highest honors one can receive in the entertainment industry. It is also a chance for celebrities to wear designer clothes that are impossible to sit in, and then sit in them for three hours. Here in Canada, the Canadian Screen Awards, or CSAs, are the equivalent of the American Oscar and Emmy, depending on whether you work in film or television. Typical of most things in Canada, it is a much smaller affair than that of our American counterparts, with a tinier budget, less hoopla, and way less jewelry.

Regardless, as a proud writer and story editor for reality television, it had always been my dream to be nominated. Moreover, I always imagined exactly how it would happen. The morning the nominations were announced, I would wake up, jump in the shower, and by the time I toweled off, I would glance at my phone, which would be blown up with supportive texts, congratulating me on my nomination for "Best Writing in a Reality Competition Series." At which point, I would beam with excitement and spend the rest of the day lying in bed, eating bonbons and offering *bon mots* to my fans on social media.

However, in "reality," beyond the fact that I have no fans, the morning the nominations were announced in 2019, I woke up in a terrible mood. I had already been overlooked two years in a row, and had just the previous night bemoaned to my friend, Alice, over a Manhattan (or two...okay fine, three) that I was convinced history was about to repeat itself. So on this particularly cold February morning, I was not optimistic. At eight thirty AM, my phone buzzed. It was an email from the Academy of Canadian Television and Film, informing me that a list of the nominations was now available for download. I immediately deleted the message and hopped in the shower.

At about nine thirty, as I headed to work, I received a text from Alice, which read: "The nominations are out; how's your level of anger?" At this point, I figured she had seen the list and was texting me to console me. I told her that I had not looked yet, and when she did not reply, I assumed that my worst fears were correct. So I parked the car, and with a dark cloud hanging over my head like a black umbrella on a foggy London day, I strode into work.

When I entered the office, the place was abuzz with talk of the nominations, which only served to further darken my mood; and avoiding all eye contact, I skulked to my desk without a word. For the next half hour, I tried to block out the cacophony of excitement around me, with the aid of a pair of ear buds and an overly exuberant interviewee on screen, while I sank deeper into a bog of despair.

At around ten thirty, my phone buzzed. It was a text from one of my editor pals with whom I had worked on a number of shows over the years, which read: "Congratulations!!!! Love you to the moon and back!! You freaking deserve this recognition so much!!!" And yes, they used that many exclamation points. I was floored. I wrote back frantically: "Are you fricking kidding me???" To which she replied, "Nope, I'm not—it's true!" Immediately, I burst into tears, overwhelmed that something I wished for had actually come true. Moments later, I received a stream of congratulatory messages, and a number of my co-workers came up to my desk and congratulated me in person. It was one of the best moments of my life, as it was exactly what I had always wanted to happen, even if it did not happen exactly how I wanted it to. I had imagined vague details about this situation, but I did not take the time to clearly visualize exactly how I wanted it to unfold.

However, even though I visualized being nominated for the Canadian Screen Awards, it never crossed my mind to consider how it would feel to win. I also had not considered what it would feel like to lose either. I really had not thought about anything. It was not until they began to read out the nominees for my category that I suddenly realized, "Ohimygawd, if I win, what am I going to say?"

So I sat there immobilized by fear, with my heart pounding a million miles a minute. I have to admit that the larger part of me in that moment hoped that I would lose, because I was so incredibly ill prepared for the alternative. Well, as they say, be careful what you wish for, as the predominant part of my thoughts won out, and I lost the award. So as I watched in false mirth, my rival leap to the stage and shriek their victory cry, a deep wave of disappointment washed over me and flung me onto the jagged rocks of my inner misery beach. Yes, whoever coined the phrase, "It's an honor just to be nominated," is a perennial optimist, because even though it is just an award, there is something about losing that triggers your inner disheartened child. The question becomes, what would have happened if I had visualized winning? How would this have affected the outcome?

Luckily and very gratefully I was a given a second chance. The following year I was nominated again and this time I decided that I would allow myself the luxury to imagine what it would actually feel like to win. So I visualized myself arriving at the venue, chatting with colleagues, drinking the tepid overly sweet white wine and ultimately, my name being called. I then mentally rehearsed how it would feel to stand in front of a crowd and deliver an acceptance speech. At that point, I will not lie; the primary emotion I registered was abject terror. So I decided that I would have to go as far as writing a speech in advance and rehearse it just so I could soothe that feeling as you always want your visualizations to based on the light emotions and not the dark ones. By the time mid-March rolled around I was ready to go. However, fate intervened and due to the global pandemic the awards were canceled and rescheduled two months later as an online presentation. Well, this immediately solved my public speaking night terrors and as luck would have it, this time it was my name that was called. This was a double blessing for not only was I thrilled to actually have won something for the first time in my life, but also it confirmed for me that positive visualization could lead to positive results.

"Weird" Science

The idea of visualization as a means to achieve your goals is not by any stretch a new concept. In 1960, Maxwell Maltz wrote, *Psycho-Cybernetics*, in which he developed techniques for improving your self-image as a way to invite success into your life. One of these ideas was visualization. A quick search on the Internet also reveals numerous sources that support visualization as a necessary tool to accomplish your goals. So how does it work? Let's take a brief look at the science behind it—"visualization for dummies," if you will.

Scientists have demonstrated that the same areas of the brain are engaged when you visualize an action as when you perform that same action in actuality. For example, it is well known that many elite athletes will not only work hard on the physical aspects of their sport but will also spend a substantial amount of time visualizing those same actions, as it has been proven that the brain cannot tell the difference between the two activities. In fact, it has been demonstrated that when an athlete imagines the physical sequence

Visualization

of events needed for their sporting event, the same muscles will fire in their bodies as if they were actually doing it. In addition, other studies have shown that when stroke victims visualize the limb or limbs that are addled in motion, they actually send blood to that part of the brain that has been damaged, and this can in turn help to repair it.

What it comes down to is that the brain does not differentiate between a real memory and a visualized one. So if you can vividly create a picture in your mind of a future desired action or state, then your brain will register this as something that you have already experienced, and therefore is possible.

The reason this works is because of your Reticular Activating System (RAS), a diffuse set of neural pathways that mediate your behavior. Your RAS is a complex network in your brainstem that filters out unnecessary data so that only the important information gets through to you. Otherwise, you would be overwhelmed by the amount of information that is constantly bombarding you. So through visualization, you have the ability to help reprogram your RAS to only accept bits of information that are important to your goals, and to separate out those bits of information that are either unnecessary or are getting in the way. Essentially, it is a positive mindset filter that can help you to develop and reinforce real skills by visually practicing them in tandem with actual physical practice. Obviously, you cannot become a competitive figure skater if you have never actually skated, but theoretically as a beginner, you can improve your physical skill level at skating, through the use of visualization. The key to this is that the more vividly you can imagine the scene or desired state of being, the better it will be recorded in your mind as an actual memory, and therefore improves your chances of making it a reality.

In addition, there are a number of benefits associated with visualization that can really help to improve your quality of life. It stimulates your creative subconscious to generate ideas to help you reach your goals. It helps to reprogram your mind to search out important resources that are essential to your success. It can help to trigger the law of attraction, build and fortify your personal motivation levels, and can even be employed to rethink your past memories and negative experiences to help you to forgive yourself. You can, in fact, use visualization as a therapeutic method to replay past experiences and responses, and develop newer, more favorable reactions to the same situations. The more I learn about it, the more it seems like a psychological cure-all, kind of like the "vitameatavegin" tonic that Lucille Ball drunkenly hawked on the "I Love Lucy" show back in the late 1950's.

See It, Say it, Do it

Visualization is an important tool in order for you to achieve your dreams and a desired state of being, so how has visualization shown up in your life? What part has it played for you in achieving success? What was the effect of your visualizations? What kind of technique(s) have you used to visualize? If all of this is new to you, there are a number of ways that you can access and practice your visualizations.

1) Mental Rehearsal

This is a three-step process that allows you to use your imagination to perfect or improve a skill that is important to you.

Step One:

Find a calm, relaxing space, and close your eyes. Now imagine you are sitting alone in a movie theatre. This eliminates the annoying potential seat kickers and chronic texters that seem to litter movie

Visualization

theatres these days. You can also omit the car commercials and trailers, and skip straight to the feature film. However, feel free to bring along popcorn or any of your other favorite refreshments, because the film you are watching is the activity that you want to do perfectly. Your task is to see yourself on the large screen, going through the step-by-step process of what it is you want to accomplish. Take in the entire picture, and consider where you are, what is happening around you, and what you look like doing the activity. After you have clearly established these details, move on to the next step.

Step Two:

This is now your chance to join the movie and become the megastar you have always been, but I would avoid the plastic surgery because everyone on the Internet is always so cruel about it—just ask Renee Zellweger. So get up from your seat, walk up to the screen, and climb inside the film. Put yourself inside of your screen self, so that you are now looking at everything from the point of view of your character on screen. Now imagine going through this same activity as you are performing it on screen. Once you have a clear sense of how this feels from your own point of view, you are ready for the final step.

Step Three:

It's time to leave your Oscar-worthy performance behind, separate yourself from your onscreen persona, and head back to your seat. Once you've sat back down and casually placed your chewing gum under the seat as a gift for the next patron, it is time to imagine shrinking the screen in which you are still performing this activity, down to the size of a soda cracker, or ginger snap if you have more of a sweet tooth. Then take your cracker or cookie, and eat it, chew it, and swallow it, so that every piece of that imagery gets absorbed into every cell of your body, and that image becomes an integral part of you. Once you feel you are full to the brim, then open your eyes and continue with your day.

This entire process should take about five to ten minutes, and through commitment and repetition, it can lead to solid results.

2) Goal Pictures

If movies are not your thing, then you can also try using specific imagery or goal pictures. The most common form of this is the Vision Board, which was popularized in Rhonda Byrne's treatise of the law of attraction, *The Secret*.

The concept is simple; you gather up images from magazines (if you can find any these days), newspapers, and our ubiquitous friend, the Internet, which represent what you want to accomplish, or how you want the various aspects of your life to look. Once you have collected everything you want, you then glue them to a board and place it in a prominent spot where you can see them every day. These boards are a lot of fun to create, as they are reminiscent of those awesome collages you used to make of zoo animals back in grade one. However, if the idea of a large board of your personal aspirations makes you feel too exposed, or seems cumbersome for your personal space, another option is what I like to call the Vision Book. This is exactly the same as a Vision Board, only you take a small journal or photo album, and place the images inside. Another way to make these vision pieces even more effective is to cut out photographs of yourself and actually place them inside the images.

An additional method is to draw or sketch out your aspirations. It is not important whether or not you are a stick figure genius or a budding Picasso, because it is not the pictures that are important but the *picturing* you do in your mind while you are drawing that helps strengthen these notions. The idea behind all of these goal pictures is that if a picture is worth a thousand words, than a visualized image is far more effective than a wordy explanation, and if you can picture it, than it can become a reality. Once again, the key is to look at it daily for it to really take hold and solidify in your mind.

3) Index Cards

If the idea of having to make a Vision Board or Vision Book is about as appealing to you as rush hour traffic on a full bladder, then another option is to write out all of your goals down on index or recipe cards. Once you have each one written out on a separate card, then every morning when you wake up, and just before bed, sit in a quiet space and read each card one at time. With each card, take twenty to thirty seconds to imagine each one of these thoughts as a reality.

4) Active Daydreaming

Now, if all of the above seem too formulaic or structured for you, then you can try what I call active daydreaming. How many times, when you were a child, were you discouraged or shamed for daydreaming, by a caregiver or teacher? I know that when I was a kid, I used to love to lie on my bed and imagine all sorts of things.

One of my favorite ones was my fantasy concert band. Yes, I was such an unbelievable geek that while other guys may have been in a fantasy hockey or football league, I created my own musical one. In my mind, I would assign the various band parts to my fellow students, and then imagine how amazing we were going to sound at the next music festival. What I did not realize at the time was that I was in effect visualizing my own success, because I always gave myself the lead clarinet parts, and two years later, without having ever taken a private lesson, I was accepted into a performance music program at university. Sure, I had practiced, but I am certain that by imagining success for the band, I inadvertently mentally rehearsed my clarinet skills. So why not sit back and just allow your mind to free-form imagine the things you would love to invite into your life? Go crazy; enjoy the freedom of just letting your mind go to those places you think are not possible. After all, daydreams can be the preview of life's coming events. The only caveat with this is that you need to be aware of your thoughts to ensure that you do not head into a negative headspace. You certainly do not want your daydreams to slide into day terrors and/or nightmares.

Are You a Good Witch or a Bad Witch?

I encourage you to explore all the above methods and figure out which one or combination works best for you. You can also supplement them with relaxation, meditation, and even hypnotherapy. It is proven that calmness during visualization increases the creativity and authenticity of the images you want to invite into your life.

The science behind this is simple, for as you relax, your brainwaves slow from beta waves to alpha waves, and sometimes even to the slower theta waves. It has been demonstrated that both alpha and theta waves are suggestible states where it becomes easier to adjust and/or reprogram your beliefs at a subconscious level. For those of you unfamiliar with the concept of hypnotherapy, it is quite straight forward: The hypnotherapist relaxes you into a deeper state of consciousness, and then offers pre-agreed upon concepts while your brain is in a more suggestible state of being. I have worked with a hypnotherapist, so presently my own visualization practice consists of a short meditation, self-hypnosis, and my own combination of mental rehearsal, index cards, and verbal affirmations. Basically, I am determined to make this work, so I am willing to do it all.

Visualization

However, one of the things that I struggle with the most is that although I seem to be quite adept at imagining all sorts of horrific worst-case scenarios, I struggle with picturing positive ones. For example, every time I get into a plane, I always imagine the floor opening up below my feet, and me plummeting to my death, so that in the end, I am a sweaty-handed bag of nerves before the plane even takes off. Now according to the neuroscientist, Dr. Rick Hansen, the reason for this is that it is programmed into our DNA that in order to ensure survival, you are hard wired to prepare yourself for the worst-case scenario. This of course made perfect sense back in the time when we needed to be constantly on guard from exterior threats in the wild; however, in the 21st century, it means that your brain has a natural way of holding onto negative experiences, and struggles to acknowledge good ones. This phenomenon, Hanson calls "negative bias." Hanson suggests that in order to overcome this, you have to actively acknowledge the good experiences to make them sink in and take hold. If this is done on a regular basis, then gradually, over time, the way your mind experiences life will change, as it has been scientifically proven that positive thoughts can actually alter the structure of our brains. This is yet another reason to pursue positive visualization, as not only will it affect the future, but it also brightens your daily perception of life.

Since these types of negative imaginings come much more easily to me than positive happy ones, I consciously make an effort to be more aware of my thought patterns, and to remember to use my powers for good and not evil. I like to use the "Wizard of Oz" theory for this, and ask myself when an image presents itself, "Are you a good witch? Or are you a bad witch?" This helps to keep me on track.

In addition, visualization is something that did not come naturally to me, so at the beginning, I set aside specific time not only to work on my actual visualizations but also to work on the act of visualization. So if you are someone to whom this concept is new, or if you struggle to visualize, then here is a five-step process that you can build upon at your own pace.

Study and memorize a photograph for a couple of minutes, then close your eyes and re-imagine the entire photograph in detail.

Once you feel comfortable with the photograph, then examine and memorize a simple object. Once you feel you have a handle on all the details of this object, once again, close your eyes and see all of it in your mind's eye.

When you have a solid grasp on how to recreate that 3D object in your mind's eye, imagine that 3D image with your eyes open, and see it interact with your environment. For example, if you have chosen a pen as your object, then imagine that pen floating through the air, landing on a piece of paper, and writing your name on the paper. Personally, I found it easier to do this part of the exercise than the first two, as putting the object into motion seems to bring it to life for me.

The next step is to think of your favorite environment or place, and imagine every single detail about it—not only how it looks but all the sounds and smells that are present. See and feel everything as if you are there and can see it from your own point of view.

Finally, imagine yourself in the above environment and then interact with it. This can mean that you touch or handle objects within the environment, and perhaps interact with other people that exist within this environment.

The key to these exercises, and any visualization, is to make sure you follow these guidelines:

Visualization

Use all your senses – see it, hear it, smell it, feel it, and in some cases, even taste it. However, if your visualization focuses on your desire to work with animals, you may want to eliminate the taste element.

It also is helpful if you attach an emotion or emotions to your visualizations, as these have been proven to improve their effectiveness. So really feel the joy, excitement, and thrill that accompany them, as the stronger the emotion behind a desired state or goal, the more likely it is to happen.

It is also important to imagine both the outcome and the process, as this will help guide you towards the desired goal or state of being.

Live and feel as if it is happening to you in this very moment; this is essential in order for it to form in your brain as a reality.

Remember that practice makes perfect. So practice, practice, practice, and rinse and repeat. Find a way to work it into your daily routine; after all, it can only improve the quality of your life.

Finally, and perhaps most importantly, expect results. It may seem obvious, but visualizations will only work if you believe them to be true. So practice believing in your dreams and yourself, and see just how far you can go.

This is something that I continue to work on because life is a continual obstacle course that you must navigate, and one of the key factors that lead towards success is perseverance; so let's find out how this plays out in your life.

Chapter Nine

Endurance

A Funny Thing Happened On the Way to the "Met"

I am one of those people who have always wanted to be able to sing. I suppose this is not an uncommon goal, since shows like American Idol and The Voice are immensely popular. There is something magical about the ability to communicate musically with our voices. It is a great skill, and even if it is not a natural talent of yours, it can be acquired to a certain extent, and I am the one who can prove it.

At a young age, my musical aspirations were quickly thwarted when in grade five, my teacher, horrified by my lack of ability, deemed it better for me to lip sync rather than sing with the class choir. So I did... and to this day, I still unconsciously mouth the words whenever I hear the dulcet strains of "The Rainbow Connection." However, that did not deter me from continuing to dream about it. In high school, I confided in one of my closest friends, Shelley, that I really wanted to sing but was terrified that I couldn't. This was a huge risk because after a rousing performance of "Memory," from Andrew Lloyd Weber's feline opus, "Cats," bizarrely as part of an Easter service at our local Catholic church, Shelley was already known in school for her natural vocal prowess. So she offered me a simple test; that is, to sing the chorus to Madonna's "Dress You Up." This not only gives you a clear indication of my age but also points to Shelley's rather pedantic taste in pop music as a sixteen-year-old. So I belted out two lines, and before I got any further, Shelley put a hand over my mouth and said, "You're right—you can't sing."

But did that stop me? Absolutely not, when I went to university, I joined the York choir and croaked my way through Mozart's Requiem, which seems rather appropriate considering I did sound a bit like a dying frog. On a side note, the highlight of that experience was that I sat next to Steven Page, long before he became a Bare Naked Lady; and in retrospect, perhaps I should have been much nicer to him. The following year, I joined a church choir and made a recording. Incidentally, I still have the "cassette," so if that doesn't date me, I don't know what would, and it was there that I was introduced to my first vocal teacher, from whom I began to take lessons.

A couple of years later, upon graduation from university, completely unsure of what to do with my life, and very much to my father's chagrin, I decided to audition for music theatre school. I can still remember standing in front of the panel of teachers, squawking out "Luck Be a Lady," like an off-key, overzealous Frank Sinatra, as they desperately tried to conceal looks of horror on their faces. Shockingly, that "lady" was lucky for me, because they granted me a spot, and to this day, I swear it was only because I am a) a male, and b) I already had a degree, coincidentally in music. However, it was not an easy go, for both my grades and my ego. In a world where the "triple threat"—that is, someone who can act, dance, and sing—was lauded, I was simply referred to as an "actor," because the other students figured that they had to give me some sort of designation, and it was painfully clear that I was not a dancer or a singer. So I kept taking vocal lessons.

When I failed my first year college singing course, I kept taking lessons.

When I dropped out of theatre school and formed a comedy troupe, where once again I was in a position where I had to sing, I kept taking lessons. And when I overheard audience comments about my inherent lack of singing ability, I kept taking lessons. However, a few years later, one night after a show, an audience member came up to me, gave me a bear hug, and blurted out, "Wow, they said you couldn't sing, but you know what? They're wrong. You actually can." Okay, this is not exactly a five-star review, but after twenty-five years, I found it to be a strong validation of my ever-persistent struggle to learn.

At this point, I am well aware that I will never be a recording artist, and no one would ever pay to hear me in concert, but most would agree that now I can carry a tune, I can hold a note, and sometimes I am even mostly on pitch. This is a huge accomplishment for me, and one that I hold dear to my heart, because I did it for me and only me, and as a result, it gives me great joy. I can now proudly say that I have performed for literally thousands, well at least in my mind. My shower and my car make excellent venues.

Obstacles and setbacks are an inevitable part of life. I have experienced them in my personal life, my educational journey, and more recently in my writing career. What I have discovered is that it is not the setbacks that are the biggest problem but how you choose to deal with them. What about you? What kinds of obstacles have shown up in your life? How have you dealt with them? What have you done or not done in order to endure? How would you like to be?

Persistence Makes Nearly Perfect

There are many aspects of life that you cannot control. So what are the factors that you actually can?

Hard work

I am a firm believer that if you work hard at something, eventually it will pay off. This does not mean that it will not be a struggle. It just means that if you truly want something, then you have to keep at it; although you must be aware that sometimes it does not always pay off in the manner in which you may have expected. I have also noticed that it is usually at your breaking point that you will see a shift—perhaps this is why it is often called a "breakthrough." I guess it's better than calling it a breakdown.

How many tales of actors have we heard, where they suffered numerous rejections before they actually succeeded? An actor friend of mine once said that acting is ten percent talent and ninety percent determination. For example, apparently, teen idol, Luke Perry, auditioned for two hundred and fifty-six acting jobs before he was offered his first gig. Now that is a clear example of someone determined to succeed.

Flexibility

However, sometimes when you work really hard, you discover that your original goal is not exactly what you actually want. So being open to change during the process is an important aspect of endurance. Even if we look to the most basic human concept of "survival of the fittest," it is the species that was able to adapt to their surroundings and change accordingly that endured. So for example, in my own career journey, I started off by going to school for music and acting, and then ended up as a talent agent, then moved into script writing. This then morphed into being a story editor/producer for reality television, and in recent years, I added becoming a coach and acting into the mix. My career path is now a conscious combination of all of the above, and a direct result of my acceptance of both change and possibility. So when you look to your future, it helps to look beyond the obstacles, and to search for the opportunities.

Mindset

One of the ways that will help you to be open to change and see the possibilities that exist, is the mindset that you approach each situation you face. In coaching, we separate the mindset into two separate categories: the "judger" and the "learner." The judger mindset is your critical mind at work, and often it is the voice of your inner critic that is determined to keep you in your place and judge how you and others handle circumstances. The opposite of the "judger" mindset is the "learner" mindset, which approaches each new situation or problem with curiosity and searches for opportunities for growth. So which of the mindsets do you generally approach life with? If you are unsure, here is an example to help you to determine this.

You really want to explore creative writing, so you sign up for a course at your local college. At your first class, the instructor asks you to write a short story about a moment from your childhood that had a strong impact on the rest of your life. So you go home, you sit down, and you access your internal Ernest Hemingway or Margaret Atwood to write what you consider to be simultaneously both a heart breaking and heartwarming story, a little part of your soul that you cannot wait to share with others. The following week, when you present this incredibly personal piece to your class, the other students and the instructor offer you feedback on how to improve your writing. So how do you receive this feedback? Is your initial reaction to berate yourself and tell yourself that you failed? Or do you take a more defensive approach and tell yourself that the instructor is an idiot, and the only reason that they are teaching the course is because they failed as a writer themselves? After all, those who cannot "do"... "teach." If so, then you are looking at the situation from a "judger" mindset.

However, if you accept the feedback with a sense of curiosity and a willingness to grow, then you are examining it from a "learner" mindset. The basic premise is that rather than criticize yourself or others for what has gone awry, the learner mindset allows you to explore the unique opportunities for growth that this particular situation allows. How you decide to look at the situation is up to you. How you react is your choice, and the one thing that you can actually control.

Accountability

Since your life is your own perception, then it is up to you how you choose to see whatever comes your way. This means that you are accountable for your own life and the choices that you make. While it is indeed true that life will continually whip logistical and emotional curve balls at you, it is your responsibility to decide how you would like to respond. In a practical sense, when you are on track to achieving a goal, and an obstacle presents itself, then you must hold yourself accountable on how you would like to overcome it. This is where the concepts of hard work, flexibility, and mindset really come into play, for they form the basis of how you will approach the problem. So whether you want to build your own house or become the next mayor of your town, and a water main bursts and floods your neighborhood, then it is how you use your hard work, flexibility, and chosen mindset that will ultimately affect the outcome.

Self-motivation

A large part of accountability is finding the inner strength to keep the train moving down the tracks, even when the ground is crumbling around you and life seems bent on sending you off the rails. There are times when you just want to shriek, in the words of Barbra Streisand and Donna Summer, "Enough is enough, I can't go on, no more, no more, no." I wish I could reassure you that this is not the case, but time and time again, you are going to face challenging situations. So there a few things that can help you keep that fire within you burning bright.

A) Enjoy the Process

For me, this is much easier said than done. I am very much a product-orientated person, so quite often I motor through tasks so that I can enjoy the fact that they are completed. If you are similar to me, then the problem with this is two-fold. First of all, there are and always will be more tasks to do, so therefore you can never actually finish your "to-do" list. Secondly, if the key to a happier and more peaceful existence is to "be in the moment," then by always looking forward to the end, you are robbing yourself of the experience of actually doing it. Although I think it is important to focus on the product, it is also necessary to try and find the joy in your course of action. Remember, life is a journey, not a destination.

B) Avoid Comparison with Others

It has oft been said that a fast track to misery, to unhappiness and discouragement, is comparing yourself to others. You must always remember that you do not know what the other person's journey in life is truly like. I am sure that you have seen the videos that show the discrepancy between how people portray their lives on social media, and what their life is actually like. Remember that there will always be people that have it better than you, and those that are worse off than you. It is in your best interest to have both compassion for yourself and those around you, as this is the road to self-care and true fulfillment.

C) Deal with Your Inner Critic

On a more practical note, one of the most important aspects of self-care is figuring out a way to quiet those internal voices that constantly get in the way of your success. In the coaching realm, this is referred to as your inner critic. This is the voice inside your head that continually puts you down or holds you back. An effective way to help battle these negative thought patterns is to first identify what these voices say to you, particularly when you are trying to solve a problem or move forward towards your goals. The second step is to try and figure out whose voice this is and how it became part of your psychological makeup. By doing so, it can help to overcome this voice and reprogram your thought process with the help of what is often referred to as your "inner champion."

If you feel that your inner critic is getting in your way, then I would like to invite you to try an exercise, or "exorcise" in this particular case.

Exorcise Your Inner Critic

This is a simple, fun exercise that I did during my first week of training as a coach. First, find a quiet space where you can be on your own. Secondly, using whatever means you have at your disposal, be it markers, crayons, pencil crayons, construction paper, pipe cleaners, or your children's Sponge Bob Band-Aids, I want you to draw a picture of, or create a physical representation of what your inner critic looks like. Essentially, think of this as an adult psychological version of something you may have done in kindergarten, and bring the same untamed, unfettered energy of your inner five-year-old to the table. Remember, this is an exercise purely for you, not one you have to share if you choose not to, and there is no one who is going to grade it either, but feel free to put it on the fridge if you are moved to do so. For inspiration, here is the one I created in my class. Incidentally, I keep it pinned to the bulletin board next to my desk, to remind me when my inner critic threatens to pull me into its web of lies.

Once you have created an image of your inner critic, the next step is for you to name it and write down the types of messages this inner critic tells you. After this, reflect on how this voice affects you, when it affects you, and whose voice is it. These are questions that may not have easy answers, so do not stress if the answers do not come right away. Trust that the truth shall reveal itself when the time is right.

Now that you have a clearer sense of what your inner critic looks like and how it impacts your presence in the world, I want to invite you to look beyond this and create an image of your inner champion. This is the warrior that you can bring to battle your inner critic when it is trying to take you down. Here is my inner champion, a fly swatter to whack the inner critic's negative messages out of commission.

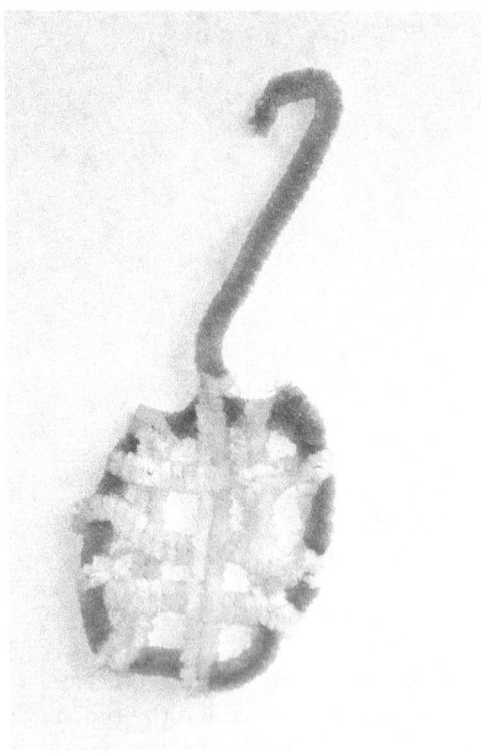

Endurance

Once again, it is important for you to remember to be patient and gentle with yourself; after all, change takes time, and these voices may have been a part of your thought process for a long time. The important thing is that you are now aware of them and how they impact your life, so you can begin to slowly take steps to move past them, and truly become the amazing human being the universe means you to be.

However, I would like to acknowledge that it is not easy. For me, these days I am aware that my inner critic voice is the loudest whenever I am an in an audition situation. In fact, sometimes my inner critic is so rambunctious that it feels like it is screaming into my ear at the top of its lungs, so that I can barely make out or comprehend what the director is telling me to do. In fact, it seems like as soon as I enter the room, my IQ drops fifty points. For example, just the other day, a director at a commercial audition very clearly asked me to start behind a table and move to a chair in the centre of the room, and then deliver my line. However, all I heard in my mind was a caveman-like chant of "chair, line...chair, line..." Consequently, it took me three times to get it right, because every time the director shouted "action," I would immediately plop myself into the chair and say, "Oh, honey...look, charcuterie on tap...this is how we do..." On a side note, it also did not help that I had no idea what the heck my line meant either, and since it was at a callback, about fifteen people who were completely nonplussed witnessed my folly.

The reason behind my struggle have both a psychological and physical basis. When you feel anxious, it triggers your nervous system to release adrenaline into your body. This rush can then override your executive function, that part of your brain that tracks information and keeps it in order.

So, I will admit that my track record with auditions has not been stellar. In fact, many of my friends ask me why I still bother, and I only have two reasons. First of all, I enjoy the adrenaline rush. Just as some people like black diamond downhill skiing, for me, auditioning offers that same type of feeling. Secondly, I am determined to be able to acknowledge this anxiety and yet still overcome it. It helps that I have never believed in the concept of the overnight sensation, as more often than not, a lot of behind-the- scenes work has gone on. I believe this concept is merely a myth that media likes to perpetuate because it makes for a great story.

Finally, and this goes for all aspects that you are trying to address in your life, *real change takes real long*. When it comes to your work or a skill you are trying to master, as Malcolm Gladwell stated in his treatise, *Outliers*, it takes about ten thousand hours or approximately ten years of deliberate practice to become an expert at anything. So continue to endure, but give yourself a break, and remember that the road to success is as The Beatles coined, "*A Long and Winding Road.*" Also, it is important to understand that not all dreams come true, at least not right away or in the way you originally imagine. After all, if they did, I'd already have an Oscar, an Emmy, and a private jet to get to my country estate, but it is imperative that you continue to strive towards them and keep an open mind. Too many people work hard for so long, only to give up just when they are about to break through. I know it's hard, but if it's important to you, then I encourage you to believe in yourself and stay on track, and that's where the true endurance comes in. In the meantime, as you persevere, it is important that you are kind to yourself. Let's now explore how you can increase this way of being, so that you can be your very best self as you continue to drive yourself towards your dream destiny.

Chapter Ten:

In the Meantime...

Tea and Lack of Sympathy

One of the unfortunate aspects of being single is that if you want to actually alter this status, then you have to go through the discomfort and sometimes complete ridiculousness of negotiating the dating world. On one of my more civilized dates—that is, at a local teashop, and a date where the person did not remark upon their return from the rest room, with surprise, "Ohmigawd, you're still here"—I discovered something important. It was during my patented "resumonologue," in which I rattle on in a rather rehearsed way about my education, my work experience, and how I ended up where I am today, always from a self-deprecating point-of-view, that I noticed my date staring at me wide-eyed with their mouth hanging open.

Me: I'm sorry, what's happening? Are you choking? Having an allergic reaction? Hibiscus tea isn't, well, everyone's cup of...tea.

Date: Um, yeah. You keep complaining about how you've never succeeded, but from what I'm hearing, you seem successful to me. In fact, I'd be super grateful if I had the career you have.

Me: Uhhhhh... What?

Date: Yeah, I think you really need to be more aware of your accomplishments, and focus less on your failures.

Me (red-faced): Uh...uh... yeah... you're right... I guess?

Needless to say, that was yet another one of my one-date wonders. It should not have come as a surprise; since life is about perception, then it would seem that I habitually chose to downplay my endeavors and up sell my failures. Attractive. Clearly, I needed a mindset shift.

Since, the road to success is riddled with many twists and turns and countless speed bumps and detours it is therefore important for you to acknowledge just how far you have come and what it is you have accomplished.

Exercise: Your Personal Accomplishment List

With this in mind I would now like to challenge you to stop and make a list of all the things you have accomplished in your life. For example, this includes everything from learning to ride a bike, right up to that promotion you may have just received the other day. So pop open that laptop, or grab that notebook— you know, the one with the rainbows, clouds, and inspirational quotes embossed on the front, like, "Do What You Love, Exceed Your Expectations, and Dream"—and start writing.

So what came up for you? What did you notice? How long is your list? What surprises you about your list of accomplishments? How often do you tend to sell yourself short? Most importantly, what is the impact of this type of behavior and mindset on your life? How would your life change if you spent more time acknowledging what you have accomplished as opposed to berating yourself for your shortcomings?

In the Meantime ...

One of the great benefits of doing this type of exercise is that it helps you to become aware of how you operate in the world, and the effect that this has, both on your daily interactions and long-term goals. Imagine how your perception of your life would change if you read your list of accomplishments everyday? In effect, by doing so, you are validating yourself, and every single person needs validation. If you are anything like me, then you may need a lot of external validation. Unfortunately, as a child, I did not receive a healthy level of external validation from my parents, as they were not capable of providing it at the time. Therefore, it has been a life-long struggle, with countless years of therapy, for me to try and learn how to self-provide what I need in order to feel safe in this world. I have also had to consciously learn how to refocus my energy, from negative to positive, on a daily basis, as I attempt to re-program what my nervous system learned at an early stage of my childhood development.

If you struggle to acknowledge yourself in a healthy way, and suffer with chronic feelings of negativity, then in addition to the above accomplishment list, I can offer a number of other options you can try in order to help shift your mindset.

A) Affirmations

A number of years ago, I was feeling completely dissatisfied with the direction that my life was heading. In addition, my writing agent at the time was pushing me to write something—"write anything" was the phrase I believe they used. Also, at this particular time, the proverbial well of my ideas for television pilots had run dry, so I tried another tactic. Since I had developed a penchant for self-help books when I worked at a bookstore in University. I was suddenly struck with an idea: what would happen if I read twelve self-help books in a year, one per month, and then wrote about my impressions of each of them on a daily basis? How would my life change? So over the course of a year, I read twelve self-help books and experimented with each of the techniques they presented while at the same time I blogged about my progress. This was of course back when blogs were still a thing, and there was one for everything, from how to clean a toilet to one written by a poodle on how to train your master. In the end, although my life changed very little over the course of that year, it did however expose me to a wide array of self-help strategies.

The very first book I chose to read was Louise Hay's, *"I Can Do It – How to use Affirmations to Change Your Life."* I use the word "read" loosely, as for this one I listened to the audio book. This was an experience in itself, as Louise read the book with more seductive tones than a Danielle Steele heroine.

In her introduction to the book, Louise outlines her basic theory that essentially boils down to: "You are what you think." Very simply put, this means that if you think happy, loving thoughts, you will feel happy and loving, and conversely, if you think nasty, horrible things, then you will feel terrible. Fair enough. Louise then goes on to state: "Think happy thoughts—it's that simple." The question that immediately popped into my mind was, if it's that simple, then why did it just take thirteen minutes for her to explain it? Regardless of this paradox, Louise went on to explain that in order to practically implement affirmations, you must follow a few simple rules:

Rule One

Affirmations must always be phrased in the present. For example, if you are looking to invite more financial security into your life, it is better to phrase it as, "I have wealth and prosperity," rather than, "One day, I'm gonna be as rich as a dyed-blonde, Texas oil wife, just as soon as I sell my one-of-a-kind, onion skin-traced Def Leppard album art on eBay."

Rule Two

The affirmation must also be phrased in the positive as opposed to the negative. So for example, if you want to bring good health into your life, you would not say, "I don't want to get sick and die," as your brain does not always register the negative, and may interpret this as, "I want to be sick." It is instead much stronger for you to say, "I want to be healthy and live a long life." In addition, this also means that when you are engaged in a *conflict resolution* discussion with your partner or housemate, you should say: "I will do my dishes with love and... sunlight," instead of, "I'm gonna break every dish in the house so that I never have to do them again."

Rule Three

You should never share your affirmations with anyone. So do not ask me what mine are; I cannot tell you. However, I will share that as a result of reading/listening to this book, I chose thirty-five affirmations that resonated with me, which I recite daily as part of my morning routine.

B) Gratitude Journal

Years ago, I encountered a great book, *The Artist's Way,* by Julia Cameron, and as with most of the self-help books I have read, I took away one major suggestion that henceforth I have regularly incorporated into my daily routine. It is the idea of "morning pages." Cameron proposes that you sit down daily and write out three, 8 1/2 x 11 pages of stream of consciousness every morning before you start your day. I imagine the principle behind this is that it stimulates your creativity, as it allows your mind to wander, and this, in theory, can potentially uncover new ideas.

Although I initially embraced this notion with vigor, over the next few years, it slowly shifted from pure stream of consciousness into a more pointed task of what I termed, "taking out the psychological garbage." So every morning, I would crawl out of bed and immediately write out every disappointment, slight, and resentment that I was experiencing. In effect, my morning pages morphed from a creative expression intended to expand my horizons, into a long-winded list of complaints and small miseries. In a nutshell, I started every day by sowing the seeds of negativity. It took me many years of low-level unhappiness to realize that by continually dwelling on the negative aspects of my life, I was re-enforcing them and weaving them deeper into the fabric of my psychological outlook.

It was not until one random evening, where among the cacophony of Argentinean Tango and the clink of glasses of Chilean Malbec, that I became embroiled in a heated discussion about the concept of the morning pages, with a woman who I found to be simultaneously aggressive and yet incredibly insightful. When I rather proudly explained that I had found a practical use for them, this woman looked at me as if I had just announced that my romantic interest was an alien being from Jupiter, and asked me point blank, "Aren't you just strengthening your negative thoughts by giving them so much weight?" Well, naturally, I was incensed—how dare she question my good sense? However, the next day, it suddenly hit me, and I wondered aloud, much to the disconcertment of those around me on the subway platform, "What if I, every morning, instead of concentrating on the bad parts of my life, shift my focus to the good parts? How would that change my perception of my life?"

Okay, I am not going to lie and say, "It was a miracle that instantly changed my life to the amazing!" because it was not. However, slowly (and I would like to emphasize the slow aspect of this process), it has gradually become easier for me to focus on the positive aspects of my life, and to allow the droning of the negative thought symphony to play second fiddle.

In the Meantime ...

So if this is something that you struggle with as well, then my best suggestion to you (which has even been sanctioned by the goddess of talk TV, Oprah) is to figure out a way to focus daily on the things in your life that you are grateful for. There are many ways you can approach this, and I believe you should pick the one that works best for you. Whether you choose to daily write out three to five aspects of your life that you are grateful for, or say them aloud regularly, it has been proven to increase your quality of life. You can even go so far as to write one long master list of all the things in your life that are wonderful or special, and then focus on some of them each day. It really does not matter how you decide to do it, but it is definitely worth the effort to try it. Believe me, you will thank yourself in the end, and maybe you can even add that to your gratitude list.

C) Meditation

Recently, one of my clients shared with me how they were completely stressed out, and that they could not figure out how to reduce the level of anxiety they were experiencing. When I asked them about what they thought was behind this unease, the client expressed that perhaps the source was that they felt a constant drive to achieve perfection in every aspect of their life. In their career, they felt they had to work harder than everyone else, put in more time, and continually approached each project with a need for it to be absolutely perfect. This same approach carried over into their personal life and their relationships. The client expressed that they felt incredibly discouraged and beaten down by life. When I offered the observation that it seemed that they were incredibly hard on themselves, the client stopped for a second and then quickly went back to their pre-determined narrative, and the discussion moved on.

About a month later, I received a message from this same client that there had been a major shift in their life. The client stated that although it did not resonate with them at the time; during a meditation they suddenly became aware of how incredibly hard they are on themselves, and how much this affects their quality of life. As a result of this realization, the client had decided to explore meditation more deeply as a way of directly dealing with their stress levels and calming their need for perfection. This illustrates two important principles: First that when it comes to coaching, it is important that the coach holds the client as creative, resourceful, and whole, which simply means that all the answers to all your questions ultimately come from inside; and secondly, the importance of meditation in your life.

In this crazy world that you live in, it is hard not to be overwhelmed by the continual onslaught of information that is flung at you. In the last twenty years, with the rise of the Internet and social media, the amount of stimulus you encounter on a daily basis has increased astronomically. As a result, it is becoming increasingly difficult these days for anyone to maintain balance and find solace. Meditation has proven not only to reduce stress but also to increase concentration. Even a few minutes every day can be incredibly helpful. I cannot stress the importance of the self-healing properties that meditation can offer you. My best suggestion for you is that you explore mindfulness and meditation, whether in a group setting or for a few minutes on your own every morning; it is incredibly beneficial to the quality of your life. It is also important to remember that it is called a "practice" for a reason, so please do not be hard on yourself when you attempt to learn this wonderful new skill. It takes years of practice to master, but you will discover that it is well worth the time and effort.

D) Rewards

When I was in grade three, spelling excited me—yes, I was that type of annoying child who would spell out every billboard, much to the chagrin of my parents. My crowning achievement was that by age seven, I could spell the word *facetious*, and was thrilled to point out that it was one of the few words that contained all the vowels of the alphabet. This was also the same year that I discovered that announcing that "Gentalia" was the new official airline of Italy, was also a good way to get a laugh from groups of adults. Oddly, I had not learned to spell *precocious* yet.

I also loved our weekly in-class tests where we had to memorize a list of vocabulary words and their meanings. I liked it because it was concrete, black and white, and probably also because, at age nine, I already just plain liked lists. Due to my enthusiasm, I generally fared fairly well on these tests, but I was not always perfect. On the days that I received eight or nine out of ten, I would bring the test home to show my parents, and even though my score was reasonably high, my father, without fail, would always focus on what I got wrong rather than the fact that I had done well. As a result, not only did my inner critic learn that I had to be perfect all the time, I also did not learn any system in order to acknowledge my hard work. This way of thinking is a pattern that I have also observed in many of my clients.

Unfortunately, I think in our society, many of you, through both your parents and the educational system, have learned to focus on your shortcomings and not the effort or the level of relative success of your own progress. Therefore, many of you do not have any conscious system of self-acknowledgement or reward. It is very important for you to pay attention equally to, if not more to, your successes, and find a way to tangibly acknowledge them. I say "tangibly" because saying to yourself, "Wow, you did a great job," is fine, but offering yourself a concrete reward strengthens your sense of worth. I would also like to point out, as many of you may fear that this will lead to arrogance, that there is a difference between self-acknowledgement and self-aggrandizing behaviors. Self-aggrandizing comes from a place of lack and a need to prove to others that you are worthy, whereas self-acknowledgement needs no audience and is merely a way to internally validate yourself. One leads to isolation, and the other closer to others, because the more you can validate yourself, the more you will find value in others, and this will lead to an upward spiral of positivity.

So I strongly encourage you to uncover ways to validate your positive actions and hard work. From a luxury coffee to a deluxe spa, the key is to reward yourself with something that is substantial so that it really registers in both your mind and body. When I have introduced this concept in coaching conversations, many of my clients have initially expressed some concerns about feeling guilty. This of course is a programmed response that they learned in childhood. It is important to remember that you are worth it, and you are allowed to feel good and to have good things happen in your life. In addition, if you learn how to reward yourself, it makes it easier to be generous in your rewards towards others. You can think of it as the Golden Rule in reverse: "Do unto yourself so that you can do good unto others." It does seem true that charity begins at home, and everything you need to know in life, you really did learn in kindergarten.

The ultimate goal, of course, is to move towards a strong acceptance of yourself and your circumstances as they are in the present moment, while you steadfastly move towards your goals of a more desired state of being or quality of life. I recognize that this is a tricky balance; however, it is one that will make all the difference in the world for you. Once again, remember that you are and will always be a work in progress, and it takes time and a lot of effort for change to affect your life. After all, if it was that simple, and all you needed was to take a pill every day, then all of us would be more addicted than 'Neely O'Hara' in "Valley of the Dolls".

I often hear from clients that they feel it is too late for them to change, be it their careers or their life situations. However, I would like to refute that, as I know of a man who after a very successful run for twenty plus years as the head of a college program, switched careers in his late sixties to become a talent agent for actors. In addition to this, he has gone on to produce live shows, and at over eighty years old is still going strong. These days, I am now in the age range where my contemporaries are beginning to discuss what their retirement will look like. I have no intention of ever retiring. I saw firsthand what it did to my father. My dad retired from his job as a Certified Management Accountant when he was sixty-five, but then went on to work three days a week for another company as their accountant. When he finally gave that up at age seventy-five, within a year, his anxiety level increased while his physical health steadily declined. What I garnered from this was that Dad still had a ton of mental energy, but with no concrete place to focus it, he turned it in on himself and created suffering. I do not know the meaning of life, but this much I do know: Everyone needs a purpose, and it is as essential to you as water, food, and sleep. When I think of this talent agent who keeps going, well into his eighties, I cannot help but admire his strength and drive towards his purpose, and I feel I can learn a lot from him.

So as you journey towards your goals, I wish you love and much success. It is all up to you. I know that you have the strength and determination to have the life you desire. Today is the day you make the first step. Go for it. I know you can do it and, ultimately, so do you.

About the Author

In addition to being an Adler Trained Coach, Mark has 20-plus years' experience working in the entertainment industry as an award winning writer, story editor, actor, casting assistant, and producer and talent agent. As a graduate of the prestigious Canadian Film Centre Primetime Television Writing Program, Mark has worked as a writer, story editor, and producer on some of Canada's top reality programs, including *The Amazing Race Canada*, *Canada's Next Top Model,* and *Chopped Canada.* Mark has also created, written, and performed with two successful comedy troupes, produced eleven short films, and produced/written over twenty live theatrical productions. Mark loves nothing more than driving his neighbors crazy with his obsessive piano practice and penchant for singing show tunes at the top of his lungs. If you are interested in a private coaching session or one of his workshops, please go to www.forgiveorforgetitnow.com.

www.ingramcontent.com/pod-product-compliance
Lightning Source LLC
LaVergne TN
LVHW051502070426
835507LV00022B/2887